Mother Mary

Rufus Randeniya

TEACH Services, Inc.
P U B L I S H I N G
www.TEACHServices.com ● (800) 367-1844

Copyright © 2013 TEACH Services, Inc.
ISBN-13: 978-1-4796-0031-1 (Paperback)
ISBN-13: 978-1-4796-0032-8 (ePub)
ISBN-13: 978-1-4796-003 (Kindle/Mobi)
Library of Congress Control Number: 2012956077

Published by

TEACH Services, Inc.
PUBLISHING
www.TEACHServices.com • (800) 367-1844

Table of Contents

Introduction

━∽∾∿∽━

The most blessed woman in history, the woman chosen by God to be the mother to His only begotten Son needs no introduction. Christians, as well as Muslims, know who she is. God picked multiple men and women to serve as judges, kings, and prophets throughout the course of history, but only one woman received the honor of being called the mother of the Savior of the world.

She added recognition to motherhood, a position that was generally taken for granted and still is in some countries. Whether a husband toils in the field or sits behind a desk, it is nothing compared to the wife's chores at home or the responsibility of raising their children. Cooking, cleaning, washing, feeding, dressing, and sending children to school are not easy. Her work is not an eight-hour shift. Some people may not recognize the value of motherhood, but God does.

God gave Mary the important task of carrying the Son of God for nine months and then caring for Him and teaching Him God's ways. Jesus could have materialized out of thin air in the manner that angels have appeared before people, but

God chose to use a woman to bring Jesus into the world in a natural way. The childhood of Jesus, apart from the mention of his disappearance in the milling crowds that came to the temple of Jerusalem, is not recorded in Scripture. As such, Jesus could have appeared as a young man at the Jordan River when His ministry began to proclaim salvation and His mission instead of spending about thirty years in unknown obscurity and apparent poverty.

But God chose otherwise. It was also Jesus' choice to be born in a human family. That choice, too, surprises many people when they contemplate that the chosen mother of the Savior was not a princess in a palace, but a simple village lassie who had already given her heart to a poor carpenter.

The gospel of John says that Jesus was the Word: "In the beginning was the Word, and the Word was with God ... All things were made by him; and without him was not any thing made that was made. In him was life; and the life was the light of men.... He was in the world, and the world was made by him, and the world knew him not. He came unto his own, and his own received him not.... And the Word was made flesh, and dwelt among us" (John 1:1–14).

Thus John began his narration of the life of Jesus. God has no beginning or end; He is eternal. He who created the universe is greater and bigger than the universe. The distances between stars are calculated by light years—millions of light years. The light runs at a speed of 186,000 miles per second. When such seconds bundle into minutes, minutes to hours, hours to days, days to months ... to years ... our brains cannot fathom such expanses. With these examples, we see how insignificant we are to even think of those sweeping concepts. The One who was involved in creating these massive cosmic masterpieces consented to become an infant to a poor woman.

This was no accident. Many prophecies had been given about the birth of Jesus, and among them the nationality, place, and ministry of the baby to be born were prominent: "A virgin shall conceive, and bear a son" (Isa. 7:14).

The Creator, who had no beginning, experienced human birth firsthand. His mother wrapped His little body in swaddling clothes and laid Him in a manger. She lovingly cared for His needs, as did Joseph. The Son of God was dependent upon humans for food, shelter, and warmth.

When the angel visited her, Mary humbly consented to conceive this Child by the Holy Spirit. She had been preselected for this sublime event, but was informed of God's plan just beforehand. What would have happened if she had panicked and refused to accept this responsibility because she knew the law of Moses required that unmarried mothers be stoned to death?

Throughout the history of God's people, it is evident that God chose individuals for major roles in His plans and assured them success in their assigned tasks. Moses and several others thus selected hesitated to shoulder such enormous responsibilities (see Exod. 4:1). However, out of love for God they decided to follow His leading. When this exceptionally virtuous young girl heard the news that she would become an unwed mother, she was certainly startled. To us this seems unacceptable, yet it was God's plan—a virgin would conceive by the power of the Holy Spirit. If this had happened to a married woman, though, her husband would have been automatically considered the child's father.

As you continue reading, you will encounter related subjects such as the devil's first lie, "You will not die," which he has used repeatedly in a slightly different manner each time. These associated facts will be discussed because the topics are intertwined and a comprehensive understanding of basic truths is essential to a complete understanding of Mary's role.

This book is about the young woman who was chosen by God to be the mother of His Son. Could any woman be more privileged? Still, the devil recognized an opportunity to deceive the world centuries after Mary's death. As believers gradually put their faith more in tradition than on the word of God, they became ready to accept any fabrication brought forth by the equally deceived church leaders. Over time the church was prepared for a deadly deception that ensnared millions unawares. Satan, who won the world through Eve, used Mary's story to divert the entire church to the path of destruction. Although the majority of Christians have chosen to rely on shortcuts to God, there are some who have chosen to cling to the eternal truths of God's Word. These believers are referred to as the remnant church, and their steadfast determination to keep the commandments of God and the faith of Jesus is recognized in heaven.

For more information on this and other subjects, please visit 3ABN.org, watch the 3ABN television channel, or call 618-627-4651.

Chapter 1

Origins of Marian Worship

—◦/◦/◦—

Mothers of great Old Testament Bible characters shine like the stars. Their dedication and fear of God is evident in the lives of their children, who stood for God during the history of His people. Moses was an Israelite baby who should have been killed according to the Pharaoh's decree. He was born for a divine purpose, which is the reason he was miraculously spared a cruel death. His mother played a key role in bringing him up in an atmosphere fit for a leader-to-be. The mothers of Samson and Samuel had a similar influence on their sons.

During the time of Jesus, mothers brought their children to Him for healing and blessing. This was a great joy for Jesus, and He blessed them all. He knew the importance of a mother's role in children's lives and demonstrated concern for the burdens they carried. A young man was among those resurrected by Jesus, and his return to life was because of

Jesus' empathy for a weeping mother accompanying her son's funeral procession. He consoled sorrowing mothers, and He cared for His own mother in her time of grief.

"Jesus knows the burden of every mother's heart. He who had a mother that struggled with poverty and privation sympathizes with every mother in her labors. He who made a long journey in order to relieve the anxious heart of a Canaanite woman will do as much for the mothers of today. He who gave back to the widow of Nain her only son, and who in his agony upon the cross remembered His own mother, is touched today by the mother's sorrow. In every grief and every need He will give comfort and help" (*The Desire of Ages*, p. 512).

Mary, the most fortunate among women, was chosen by God for an unprecedented honor, but she has been upheld by humans as the object of highest adoration. Some of the titles given to her by her fans and followers are: Mother of the Church, First of All the Saints, Our Lady, Queen of Heaven, Mother of God, The Model Believer, The Lady of All Nations, The Guardian of the Faith, The Immaculate Conception, The Pure Sinless One, Queen of the Most Holy Rosary, Our Lady of Guadalupe, His Immaculate Spouse, The Second Eve, and The Queen of the World.

Mary's obedient, submissive demeanor was unnecessarily glorified by the Catholic Church, which crowned her as the Queen of Heaven. She lived her entire life out of the limelight only to be shamefully glorified centuries later with titles that would embarrass her; there was a Queen of Heaven among pagan deity long before Mary's time. The attempt of the church to superimpose unwarranted glory and honor upon Mary takes her out of her natural setting and credits her with qualities that she did not possess. The church portrayed her as immaculate, whereas she herself admitted her own need of a Savior (see Luke 1:47).

It is estimated that more than two billion Hail Mary's are said daily by believers. How could this happen? Who made her a mediator? Pray for us! Pray for us! Pray for us! Billions of people are urging her to pray for them. All the "saints" are petitioned for prayers for the believers. These are vain attempts to gain favor from the dead, while Jesus, the only living Mediator, the Truth and the Way, is sidelined.

The subject of adoration seems to produce divided opinions. The stand of the Catholic Church regarding Marian adoration is clear; the Catholic Church is openly opposed to the adoration given to Mary and states that the saints are not supposed to be adored or worshipped. However, this has become a problem for church administrators. Adoration belongs only to God, yet it is hard to separate those Catholics who adore Mary from those who do not. Saints are venerated, although nearly all who look to the images of saints have no clear understanding of the difference between adoration and veneration. This class of "saints," which is a production of the Catholic Church, needs no veneration as they are not real saints. I define them as a class of saints, because the Bible identifies the saints as those who "keep the commandments of God, and have the testimony of Jesus Christ" (Rev. 12:17). Commandment keepers do not worship idols or pray to saints.

According to the entry on idolatry in the Catholic Encyclopedia, the Catholic believer knows or is supposed to know "that in images there is no divinity or virtue on account of which they are to be placed in them." This encyclopedic view is not apparent among the worshipers who hug, kiss, and worship the statues of saints. Idol worship begets other sins that debase human dignity, and we may confidently guess that the excessive indulgence of idolatry was the source of Sodom and Gomorrah's great depravity.

Jesus won the hearts of those who listened to Him. They were touched by the words He spoke. One woman praised the mother of this wonderfully eloquent young man by exclaiming: "Blessed is the womb that bare thee" (Luke 11:27). Jesus paused for a moment in His discourse, and His immediate reply was: "Yea rather, blessed are they that hear the word of God, and keep it" (verse 28).

Why did Jesus redirect toward God the praise intended for His mother? Many believers naturally tend to praise Jesus' mother for the good they see in Him. This is normal because in any society parents are admired for the achievements of their children. That woman's response was spontaneous. Jesus was not against the word "blessed" that the woman used to describe Mary; Mary used that same word to describe herself. "For he hath regarded the low estate of his handmaiden: for, behold, from henceforth all generations shall call me blessed" (Luke 1:48). There is no question about her blessedness. However, one thing is made crystal clear by the reply Jesus gave to the woman: blessedness comes from hearing and keeping the word of God. Mary was qualified to be called blessed because she heard God's message and accepted it. This blessedness is infinitely greater than that of being the mother of a noble person. From a human perspective, parents are blessed by having talented and virtuous children, but the true blessedness of hearing the word of God and observing it has eternal consequences. This is what Jesus meant, and the word "rather" used by Jesus cements this notion.

From a human perspective, the terms "blessed" and "blessedness" could be applied to many of those who gave great sons and daughters to their nation, who cared for the needy on a grand scale, who donated a kidney to save a dying individual, and so on. But Jesus reserved this honorary term for a greater purpose. He was preaching about salvation, and a woman interrupted to praise the mother of the preacher. This is why Jesus said what said. He did not intend to dishonor His mother in any way; He merely refocused His listeners' attention to what He was teaching.

Observance of the Ten Commandments is emphasized throughout the Bible. Nevertheless, the Catholic Church changed these eternal commandments when errors such as idol worship and Sunday observance crept into the church. The Catholic version of the Ten Commandments is found in the Catholic Bible and the catechism books. In addition to the modified commandments, they have the Canon Law, which is comprised of 1,752 rules to deal with all Catholic faith-related matters. They emphasize that the Canon Law is more important than their revised moral law, the Ten Commandments. Those who claim the authority to modify God's law also possess the audacity to invent "saints" to mediate for believers in heaven.

My experience in Catholic education was rich in Marian worship. Our teachers, nuns, and fathers required us to pray to Mary, and in fact, we regarded her with more esteem than her Son. Annually, the entire school walked in procession to the Basilica of Our Lady of Lanka at Tewatta, which is dedicated to Mary. We chanted the Rosary as we walked two hours to our destination. Some of our teachers monitored the procession from a vehicle that went back and forth along the line of students. The dust clouds kicked up on the gravel road by more than one thousand students are still vivid in my memory. In retrospect, I try to determine if we venerated her or worshipped her. The matter was never explained to us by our catechism teachers, and I wonder if it is clear to the present generation.

If I say that the Catholic Church is Mary's church, it sounds true. There is no other church that is so historically dedicated to Marian affairs as this church. The solemn warning of Christ should be taken to heart; it is more important to be blessed by hearing the Word of God and observing it than by following blessed persons. Unfortunately, the Catholic Church upholds traditions and the word of man instead of the Word of God. They present a human ordained "ten commandments" instead of the Ten Commandments given by God.

Pharisees and scribes once came to Jesus from Jerusalem to ask a question that bothered them: "Why do thy disciples transgress the tradition of the elders? for they wash not their hands when they eat bread" (Matt. 15:2). These men came all the way from Jerusalem to ask Jesus about hand washing. Nowadays we are taught by our mothers to wash our hands before eating for health reasons, but these men were not concerned about anyone's health. They came to argue about a tradition of their elders that was being ignored, which was important because whatever the elders said to do was regarded as a decree. Since Jesus was a Jew, He was supposed to abide by the same traditions and laws.

Jesus first pointed out how these very same tradition keepers evaded the fifth commandment's requirement to honor one's parents. Under the guise of commitment to the temple, ungrateful people found a way to avoid helping their needy parents. Jesus was well aware of this sin among them, and He asked, "Why do ye also transgress the commandment of God by your tradition?" (verse 3). The tradition of the elders had created a loophole through which the cunning could escape the obligations of the commandments. With such tricks prescribed by them, it reflected what kind of elders they really were.

Jesus further stressed His point by quoting a strong statement by the prophet Isaiah: "This people draweth nigh unto me with their mouth, and honoureth me with their lips; but their heart is far from me. But in vain they do worship me, teaching for doctrines the commandments of men" (Matt. 15:8, 9).

The practice of obeying the commandments of men rather than the commandments of God has not changed over time. About 1,500 years ago, the Catholic Church presented a revised set of ten commandments, which contain stark changes from the original Ten Commandments. The modified Catholic commandments omit God's commandment that forbade idol worship. God emphasized resting on the seventh-day Sabbath in His fourth commandment, but the modified Catholic commandment leaves out any mention of the day of the week, thus opening the door for the presentation of Sunday worship based on Jesus' resurrection. When questioned, the Catholic Church acknowledges that they transferred the Sabbath from the seventh day to the first day of the week. The prophecy continues to be fulfilled: 'In vain they do worship me, teaching for doctrines the commandments of men."

With the absence of the original second commandment, the church was left with only nine commandments. The remedy for this was easily found, and the tenth original commandment was divided into two commandments. How dare they tamper with these divine commandments that God said are eternal? Compare God's ten commandments and the Catholic ten commandments.

Biblical Ten Commandments	Catholic Ten Commandments
I am the Lord thy God, which have brought thee out of the land of Egypt, out of the house of slavery. Thou shalt have no other gods before me.	I am the LORD thy God. Thou shalt have no strange gods before Me.
Thou shalt not make unto thee any graven image, or any likeness of any thing that is in heaven above, or that is in the earth beneath, or that is in the water under the earth. Thou shalt not bow down thyself to them, nor serve them: for I the Lord thy God am a jealous God, visiting the iniquity of the fathers upon the children unto the third and fourth generation of them that hate me; And shewing mercy unto thousands of them that love me, and keep my commandments.	Thou shalt not take the name of the LORD thy God in vain. (The second commandment that forbids idol worship was removed by the papacy and replaced with the third commandment.)
Thou shalt not take the name of the Lord thy God in vain; for the Lord will not hold him guiltless that taketh his name in vain.	Remember to keep holy the Sabbath day.

Biblical Ten Commandments	Catholic Ten Commandments
Remember the sabbath day, to keep it holy. Six days shalt thou labour, and do all thy work: But the seventh day is the sabbath of the Lord thy God: in it thou shalt not do any work, thou, nor thy son, nor thy daughter, thy manservant, nor thy maidservant, nor thy cattle, nor thy stranger that is within thy gates: For in six days the Lord made heaven and earth, the sea, and all that in them is, and rested the seventh day: wherefore the Lord blessed the sabbath day, and hallowed it.	Honor thy father and thy mother.
Honour thy father and thy mother: that thy days may be long upon the land which the Lord thy God giveth thee.	Thou shalt not kill.
Thou shalt not kill.	Thou shalt not commit adultery.
Thou shalt not commit adultery.	Thou shalt not steal.
Thou shalt not steal.	Thou shalt not bear false witness against thy neighbour.
Thou shalt not bear false witness against thy neighbour.	Thou shalt not covet thy neighbour's wife.

Biblical Ten Commandments	Catholic Ten Commandments
Thou shalt not covet thy neighbour's house, thou shalt not covet thy neighbour's wife, nor his manservant, nor his maidservant, nor his ox, nor his ass, nor any thing that is thy neighbour's.	Thou shalt not covet thy neighbour's goods.

The original Ten Commandments are descriptive to a point and were written by God's finger. The revised Catholic ten commandments are a brief list lacking details. The presentation of the divine law at Mt. Sinai was extremely impressive and aptly showed the importance of the law. How could men tamper with this eternal law without incurring divine curse on themselves?

"God purposed to make the occasion of speaking His law a scene of awful grandeur, in keeping with its exalted character. The people were to be impressed that everything connected with the service of God must be regarded with the greatest reverence.... On the morning of the third day, as the eyes of all the people were turned toward the mount, its summit was covered with a thick cloud, which grew more black and dense, sweeping downward until the entire mountain was wrapped in darkness and awful mystery. Then a sound as of a trumpet was heard, summoning the people to meet with God; and Moses led them forth to the base of the mountain. From the thick darkness flashed vivid lightnings, while peals of thunder echoed and re-echoed among the surrounding heights" (*Patriarchs and Prophets*, p. 303, 304).

"Whatsoever he saith unto you, do it" (John 2:5). These encouraging words were uttered by Mary at the wedding in Cana. Good advice from a mother who had complete confidence in her son. The most important request He made

during His three-and-a-half year ministry is found in the
fourteenth chapter of the gospel of John: "If ye love me, keep
my commandments" (verse 15). He was talking about His
commandments and not the ones formulated by the Catholic
Church. Loving God and keeping His commandments always
go together; these two issues cannot be separated. Those
who do not abide by the original divine commands as given
in Exodus 20:2–17, cannot say that they love God because
Jesus plainly said, "If ye love me, keep my commandments."

Jesus lived a sinless life on earth; He loved God and
lived according to the eternal commandments. It is clear that
loving God results in honoring His law and living by His commandments. A law-abiding life pleases God. Some attempt to
identify commandment keeping as legalistic or salvation by
works. Actually, there is no action involved in keeping the
law; instead it is simply living life honoring the law. We find
these words embedded in the end of the second commandment: "... and shewing mercy unto thousands of them that
love me, and keep my commandments" (Exod. 20:6).

Daniel prayed, "O Lord, the great and dreadful God,
keeping the covenant and mercy to them that love him,
and to them that keep his commandments" (Dan. 9:4). God
cares for His people, and they are identified as those "that
keep the commandments of God, and the faith of Jesus"
(Rev. 14:12).

"Satan represents God's law of love as a law of selfishness. He declares that it is impossible for us to obey its precepts. The fall of our first parents, with all the woe that has
resulted, he charges upon the Creator, leading men to look
upon God as the author of sin, and suffering, and death. Jesus
was to unveil this deception. As one of us He was to give an
example of obedience. For this He took upon Himself our nature, and passed through our experiences. 'In all things it

behooved Him to be made like unto His brethren.' Heb. 2:17"
(*The Desire of Ages*, p. 24).

Jesus' example showed that a law-abiding life in this
world of temptations is possible through the power God has
made available to us. Our heavenly Father gave us ten rules
that cover everything pertaining to life in this world. He
loves to see us abiding by them, and obedience to His commands displays our love for Him.

This is an eye opener to all who call themselves Christians.
There is a stark difference between God's people and those
who are not. All these people are mixed in Christendom like
wheat and tares in a field. They look alike, but at the harvest
they are separated. Some will be taken indoors while others
will be cast into the fire (see Matt. 13:24–30).

Yes, there are two classes of Christians in the world. Of
the billions who call themselves Christians, only some have a
distinct concept of what they believe and how to live based on
that belief. Others are not sure of most of the basic dogmas
of their faith, and they carry on a generally religious life as
lightly as possible. These men and women are like tares in
the Lord's field. Religion for them is just like a party affilia-
tion. Even in political parties, there are some who are active-
ly engaged with their party's ideals, while others just hang
on to the party symbol. These latter individuals are floaters
who can drift away easily to another party. Because they
hold party policies lightly, party leaders don't count much on
these passive folks.

Jesus looked up to heaven and prayed to His Father before His betrayal, "I have manifested thy name unto the men
which thou gavest me out of the world: thine they were, and
thou gavest them me; and they have kept thy word.... I pray
for them: I pray not for the world, but for them which thou
hast given me; for they are thine" (John 17: 6, 9).

Jesus prayed for His disciples, those who were given to Him by the Father. They originally belonged to the Father and were given over to Jesus. This brings to light a fact about the Father—He knows His people. The billions of people teeming on this earth are not all His, but He knows His people wherever they are. The Father has multitudes scattered all over the earth who need further guidance and saving knowledge. Such are given to Jesus and are provided opportunities to become strong in faith. Praise God as you become aware of spiritual things because He is the One guiding you to a saving knowledge of Himself.

The Bible speaks of two classes of believers who live on this earth. These two classes have existed from the beginning of human history. One class possesses a clear view of faith-related matters while the other class sees them as insignificant and vague. Even in the future, these two classes will exist as they are.

This second group of believers is made up of non-committed Christians in the church. A shifting, a great shaking, is coming. A fig tree is shaken violently to harvest the figs. Many of the figs fall off the tree, but a few remain attached to the branches. A shaking in the church is anticipated, and I see it already in progress. Those who are not strongly attached to the tree are falling away because of the shaking that comes in the form of temptations, allurements, discouragement, and selfishness.

Some of God's people are in the church, and some are not. They may be affiliated with other religions or living with no attachment to any religion at all. His people recognize His calling, though, just like our pets come when we call them. I have noted this with fascination. My eldest son was six years old when a neighbor gave him a baby chick. He named it Attikikily, and he fed and cared for it well. Whenever my son called "ba ba ba," the chicken always made a beeline for him, but none of the neighbors' chickens came with it.

Once I held an evangelistic meeting in my church for ten days. I went all over the village distributing hundreds of handbills. As I was walking down a narrow trail, I came across a teenage girl draping washed clothes over the fence to dry in the sun. I told her about the meetings, and she came in the evening. She continued to attend, got baptized at the end with several others, and after twenty-four years I still thank God for her faithfulness. She was one of several who accepted the truth, but her prompt response was like those disciples who followed Jesus without hesitation when He called them.

This is how God's people respond as they encounter the gospel of salvation. Through the centuries God has directed His people to truth, which has been proclaimed by teachers and preachers, and broadcast by other effective media such as the printed word and now radio, television, and the internet. Whether they identify with a particular religion or not, His people hear His voice and take action. God is calling at this late hour, "Come out of her, my people" (Rev. 18:4). I cannot overemphasize the need to return to a faith that withstands all challenges, that makes positive changes to receptive hearts.

God's people cling to the divine law, and their love for Him is reflected in a life of obedience. Others casually accept an amended law given to them by their spiritual mentors, as is demonstrated by many who call themselves Christians.

The official title given to Mary by the Catholic Church is *Theotokos*. In early centuries the Catholic Church had a problem defining the true nature of Jesus and the nature of Mary. Some could not reconcile the fact that Jesus was both human and divine. They saw Him behaving as a man seemingly devoid of divine power—He was angry, thirsty, sorrowful, and argumentative, and He cried out for the cup to be removed from Him if possible. In AD 431 the Council of Ephesus declared that Jesus is truly God and truly man and proclaimed that Mary is the mother of God, *Theotokos*. In this way Mary became known as "mother of God," though she had been commonly known as "mother of Jesus."

In order to establish the divinity and the humanity of Jesus as inseparable virtues, the church thought it was essential to grant Mary divine status, thus designating her as both human and divine as well. Whenever the church confronted a dilemma concerning Mary, a council convened for that purpose stood up for her. Unfortunately the conclusions drawn by these councils were mere speculations in most cases. It is recorded in some Catholic books that "it was believed that Mary was taken up body and soul by God to reign in heaven." Known as the Assumption, this belief has become a Catholic doctrine. The very word "assumption" reveals that this concept is somewhat of a guess. "Queen of Heaven" was another title given to her and these titles are effective only within Catholic confines. Believers of many other faiths, except Islam, give a feminine face to their spiritual gurus. As for the Catholics, Mary is the feminine face of God; a very powerful saint who is able to dictate terms in heavenly courts.

The Roman Empire was permanently divided into two kingdoms after the death of the emperor Theodosius in 395. By this time the eastern half was much stronger than the western half, which was ruled by Rome. The eastern empire was more important to Christianity primarily because the majority of churches initiated by the apostles were in this part of the former Roman Empire. This priority is observed in the fact that all ecumenical councils were held in the east. The tug of war between the Roman Latin Christianity and the eastern Byzantine Greek Christianity is obvious in church administrative affairs and is visible in the division between the Roman Catholic Church and the Orthodox Church. As Roman imperial power began to wither away, bishops emerged as managers of the kingdom, which paved the way to the papacy as foretold in prophecy.

The seeds of Christianity planted in Egypt grew into a strong church in its own right. An early apostolic visit to Egypt had illuminated the inhabitants with the message of the salvation. This church is known as the Coptic Church, which has her own pope in Egypt. It is thought that the believers in the Egyptian church first developed the concept of "mother of God" because of the traditional Egyptian belief about the goddess Isis. The goddess Isis had dominated the Nile Valley traditional worship rites for more than four thousand years. Statues and wall paintings depict the virgin Isis with her baby, Horus. The holy mother and son concept and the virgin Isis conceiving Horus were already part of Egyptian legend. The similarities between this mother and son pair and Mary and the infant Jesus are easily noted.

Egyptians worshipped Isis as the mother of a god, and for those who converted to Christianity, it was convenient for them to continue this cultural trend. The iconography of an infant Horus in the arms of Isis was a familiar sight to those who frequented ancient Pharoahic temples, and the solemn thought of the presence of a god increased their devotion. In fact, some Christian tourists have mistaken the depictions of Isis and Horus for Madonna and the baby Jesus. This prompted them to worship the deity portrayed in the temples of the Nile valley. It was easy to integrate this practice into a newfound faith that also had a god born of a woman.

In the first century BC, Egyptian culture—the Alexandrian culture to be more precise—influenced the

Roman Church before it even existed. Romans Julius Caesar and Mark Antony and the Egyptian Cleopatra amalgamated these differing cultures, which had strong implications on the beliefs of these two powerful nations. The Coptic Church bequeathed the "mother of god" sentiment that the Roman and Orthodox churches naturally and logically accepted. This idea belatedly exalted Mary to unwarranted heights and created a worship system of saints in which billions are ensnared. Thus Mary became the Isis of the modern Christian faith. For these billions of believers to escape this snare, it is imperative that they discern the truth concerning idol and saint worship.

The Dublin-based Legion of Mary is an association of Catholic laity. This Mary's army has been called "a miracle of these modern times." They encourage lay members to pray to Mary daily. The legionaries say, "Mary stands on the world globe, with her feet crushing the head of the serpent, the devil, as was announced in Genesis...." This statement is a lie. You don't find in Genesis an announcement about a woman crushing the head of the serpent. What God said to the serpent was "I will put enmity between thee and the woman, and between thy seed and her seed; it shall bruise thy head, and thou shalt bruise his heel" (Gen. 3:15). The woman's seed, Jesus, would conquer the devil by His resurrection, thereby crushing his head.

Ancient Greeks worshipped a goddess named Artemis. This Hellenistic goddess was known later among the Romans as Diana. Both of those nations attributed some special qualities to this goddess, among which was her presence with them in the hour of death. This thought was seamlessly transferred to the Marian veneration, and devotees pray for Mary's help in the hour of their death by means of a phrase incorporated in the Hail Mary prayer:

"Hail Mary, full of grace,
The Lord is with thee;
Blessed art thou amongst women,
And blessed is the fruit of thy womb, Jesus.
Holy Mary, Mother of God,
Pray for us sinners,
now and at the hour of our death. Amen."

Mary is the mother of the church according to Catholics. In the first century, when the disciples were preaching the gospel of Jesus Christ, there was not a mother of the church, nor were there any Catholics. Marian feasts were held much later when the clear perception of pure doctrine was waning. Error crept in to fill the vacuum left behind by removal of the truth. Time and again Satan has introduced substitutes to claim the worship of men, but God's law stands firm: "I am the Lord thy God.... Thou shalt have no other gods before me" (Exod. 20:2, 3).

Here Satan introduces Mary's honored calling as a potential challenge to God's command. Yet who would speak against her position? Who would dare belittle her? She was the mother of Jesus. But Mary, who had no place in the gospel message that Jesus was the Christ, the Messiah who died for the sins of the world, was thrust into the spotlight. The spiritual burden of the early inspired preachers was to present Jesus to the world and they liberally used His teachings to convince their listeners. All that mattered was this man called Jesus Christ who was the son of God, not the woman who gave birth to Him. The apostle Paul used the word "virgin" in sermons and epistles to present his view of different subjects, but he was not referring to Mary or to the birth of Jesus (see 1 Cor. 7:28, 34, 36, 37; 2 Cor. 11:2).

Marian adoration and veneration has exceeded ethical limits in some areas of the world. The learned and cultured societies know their boundaries and know that worship belongs only to God. This knowledge is not found in communities in which the level of literacy is low. The way they regard Mary is obvious by their excessive dedication and devotion to the mother of Jesus. Such individuals are not in a position to differentiate worship from veneration. Therefore, the answer to the question "Do you worship Mary?" varies according to the person questioned.

Listeners were touched by the apostles' message and most accepted Jesus as their Savior. They saw Him as God's Son. That was what mattered, not details about His mother, father, family members, and birthplace. Foreign dignitaries come to our eastern country every now and then. We welcome them on red carpets and listen to them. We don't bother to find out about their parents' professions or where they attended high school. Likewise, it simply didn't occur to the early Christians to worry about the parents of Jesus.

Maryam and her son Isa in the Qur'an are the Mary and Jesus of the Bible. Both Islamic tradition and Christian belief hold that Mary was a virgin when she gave birth to Jesus. However, the spiritually dead Roman Church set Mary on a pedestal by stating that she was the "mother of God," an important person who deserves recognition. Some believers are very fond of Baby Jesus, an image that Satan likes to promote. Mary is the young, strong mother, and Jesus is just a helpless baby dependent upon His mother. There are people who think of Jesus as a helpless babe still in the supportive arms of Mary. The psychological effects of this view of Jesus are a great reverence for and trust in Mary, and the believer becomes governed by emotions rather than by sound doctrines.

To obtain a better understanding of Mary, many scholars have painstakingly conducted research to learn about
the religious, economic, cultural, and political environs of the
Holy Land that existed 2,000 years ago. Yet the general concept of Mary is merely a reflection of pretty pictures and the
material taught in catechism classes. Medieval artists painted her as a very attractive lady out of awe and respect for
her. But do these serene images portray the real Mary who
brought up our Lord and Savior Jesus Christ? Choose any
photo of a Palestinian woman dressed in everyday clothes
and compare that picture to the paintings of Mary. There
will be a stark contrast between the depictions of Mary and
the average Palestinian woman. Mary was not necessari-
ly a beauty, although many prefer to think of her as such.
Jesus didn't even appear as the handsome and awe-inspiring
pre-incarnate Michael (see Dan. 10:13, 21; 12:1). There was
nothing special about His looks; He was just another young
man among all the others (see Isa. 53:2).

Mary's real name was Miryam, a common name that
was passed down through the generations because of Moses'
sister, Miriam. Her birthplace is thought to be the small
village of Nazareth, a notorious town known for its wicked
inhabitants. There are villages in Asian countries now that
are avoided by the neighboring peoples for the same reason.
Mary was a girl who feared God despite this challenging en-
vironment. Those who lived outside of Nazareth condemned
this village and its people. They could not accept the idea
that the Messiah would come from Nazareth. They mocking-
ly asked: "Can there any good thing come out of Nazareth?"
(John 1:46). The young man Jesus, who grew up in this village, would have been regarded by many with disdain. Yet
beautiful water lilies grow in muddy marshes.

Mary spoke Aramaic, and Jesus learned this language

from her. Jesus used this language openly as we see in the gospel record: "Eli, Eli, lama sabachthani" (Matt. 27:46). Jesus grew up in a culture that utilized many languages and would have been exposed to Hebrew in the synagogue and to Latin and Greek, which were spoken by Roman soldiers and high-class traders. However, historians express doubt concerning the ability of Mary to read and write since illiteracy was common among the women of her day.

"Angels attend Joseph and Mary as they journey from their home in Nazareth to the city of David. The decree of imperial Rome for the enrollment of the peoples of her vast dominion has extended to the dwellers among the hills of Galilee. As in old time Cyrus was called to the throne of the world's empire that he might set free the captives of the Lord, so Caesar Augustus is made the agent for the fulfillment of God's purpose in bringing the mother of Jesus to Bethlehem. She is of the lineage of David, and the Son of David must be born in David's city" (*The Desire of Ages*, p. 44).

When Mary and Joseph traveled to Bethlehem for the Roman registration of tax payers, Mary was a young woman in the advanced stages of pregnancy. This was a strenuous journey that took several days, and she would have walked or ridden a beast of burden. Many young women in Palestine were given in marriage between the ages of thirteen and fifteen. If Mary was about fifteen years old when she conceived by the power of the Holy Spirit, she would have been around forty-five years old when Jesus died. The Bible records her presence at the foot of the cross and in the upper room at Pentecost, but does not mention her again after this event.

Some believe that John, to whom Jesus gave charge of Mary before He died, took her to Ephesus, which is in modern Turkey. This city was famous for another well-known goddess named Artemis. When Paul went to Ephesus, he personally witnessed people worshipping Artemis. The traditional belief that Mary lived in Ephesus has no reliable proof.

There is no biblical record of Jesus referring to Joseph during His earthly ministry. By the time Jesus commenced His public ministry, Joseph had probably died. During His years at home, though, Jesus and His brothers must have worked alongside their father to help support the family. One can imagine how Jesus may have helped His carpenter father. Logs had to be secured, brought home, and stacked to be used for lumber. Saw blades and chisels needed to be sharpened often. These would have been the tasks of Joseph's helpers. Carrying cut lumber and delivering completed items to customers would have been constant activities.

Mary, as the wife of a hard-working husband and the mother of several children, must have been quite busy at home. She maintained a low profile as did Joseph for we do not read about anything out of the ordinary in their family. Mary and Joseph would have been keenly aware of the circumstances surrounding the beginning of Jesus' life during the early years of their marriage. "This child is God's Child," they must have reminded themselves often.

This awareness mingled with respect is obvious in the biblical record of their breathless search for Him when He was twelve years of age. After realizing that He was not with them on their way home to Nazareth from Jerusalem after Passover, both of them came rushing back to find Him. They were frightened because of the immense responsibility they bore for this Child. Yet as they approached Him in the temple, they spoke with controlled anxiety. If my father and mother had found me in that situation, the first thing I would have expected from them would be instant punishment for my wayward behavior. Their respectful response at that moment must have been how they treated the Child throughout His life. Yes, Mary was the most blessed mother of this Son of God, Jesus Christ. But we dare not call her the mother of God for she does not hold the position of mother of God. This is blasphemous and unacceptable.

The mother of god or mother goddess concept was a vital part of ancient mythology. These mother goddesses had different names in various cultures. The people worshipped their gods but gave extra adoration to the god's mother under the assumption that the mother must be superior to the son. With this established pattern of thinking, it was easy for Catholics to give additional veneration to Mary.

It's not hard to see the practicality of this rationale. In our Asian country, we had very difficult times during the reign of some prime ministers during the 1960s. At that time, the president was just a ceremonial figure and the executive leader of the country was the prime minister. Thousands of people were jobless, and frustration led to revolutions. It was not easy to access the prime minister, who could easily give a note granting power of employment in the government sector. Many people attempted to gain access to a family member of the prime minister to get the desired favor. Likewise, if one thinks it is hard to get to a god, why not try a shortcut? The god's mother must have more power than the god, according to human thinking. One could also expect some leniency from a mother figure, and certainly the god would not say no to a request made by his mother in behalf of some lesser being. This concept doesn't make sense when applied to the mother of Jesus. He had a human mother, but God does not. God has no beginning or end—He is eternal.

Although King David wrote most of the book of Psalms, the recognized author of Psalm 90 is Moses, the only man who encountered God face to face. His understanding of

Yahweh, the eternal God, is apparent in this very special psalm. "Lord, thou hast been our dwelling place in all generations. Before the mountains were brought forth, or ever thou hadst formed the earth and the world, even from everlasting to everlasting, thou art God " (Ps. 90:1, 2). God is self-existent, and He has no beginning or end.

The stable in Bethlehem was the birthplace of the incarnate Jesus, but it was not His beginning point. He said, "Before Abraham was, I am" (John 8:58). John also writes that Jesus was with God in the beginning (see John 1:1, 2). Therefore it is wrong to call Mary "mother of God." The Bible never uses that blasphemous term, but it correctly refers to her as the mother of the Lord (see Luke 1:43). The Lord Jesus had a human mother, but God is eternal and He is no one's son.

Chapter 2

Angelic Visit

Angels are God's messengers. The Bible records several instances when they conveyed divine messages not entrusted to the prophets. The angel Gabriel is the messenger who brought a message from God to Daniel (Dan. 9:21) and much later to John on the isle of Patmos (Rev. 1:1). Gabriel appeared to Mary and told her, "Fear not, Mary: for thou hast found favour with God. And, behold, thou shalt conceive in thy womb, and bring forth a son, and shalt call his name Jesus" (Luke 1:30, 31). Mary asked the angel, "How shall this be, seeing I know not a man?" (verse 34). The angel explained his message to her, saying nothing will be impossible with God. Mary replied, "Behold the handmaid of the Lord; be it unto me according to thy word" (verse 38).

"'His name shall be called Immanuel,...God with us.' 'The light of the knowledge of the glory of God' is seen 'in the face of Jesus Christ.' From the days of eternity the Lord Jesus Christ was one with the Father; He was 'the image of God,' the image of His greatness and majesty, 'the outshining of His glory.' It was to manifest this glory that He came to our world. To this sin-darkened earth He came to reveal the light of God's love,—to be 'God with us.' Therefore it was prophesied of Him, 'His name shall be called Immanuel.' " (*The Desire of Ages*, p. 19).

God does not make good and virtuous people, nor does He make bad ones. However, He does know the hearts of all men and women. God saw Mary's heart; there He found humility, love, and faith in Him. These qualities were not put there by God, but were present through parental nurture and development by Mary. This is what qualified her to be the mother of His only begotten Son.

We call her Mary, but that is not the name she would have heard when someone addressed her. Her native Aramaic name would have been Miryam, or Miriam. This is an indigenous Hebrew name, and she would have never known the westernized modern name "Mary." Miryam was a common name among Israelite women, which we discover in the narrative surrounding the death of Jesus; there are three women named Mary, or Miryam, mentioned.

Matthew and Luke record that Mary was a virgin when she received the message from heaven. She had already been betrothed to Joseph, a carpenter by trade. He was a man who lived by the sweat of his brow, a man who fashioned things to make others comfortable in their homes and workplaces. There is a saying in my country that there isn't a chair in carpenter's house. Carpenters have never been rich people but the furniture shop owners are a different class.

Prior to Mary and Joseph's marriage, the angel visited Mary, who probably tried to convey the message to Joseph about the miraculous conception. Her tale must have broadsided Joseph. He would have been devastated by this unexpected news, as any husband-to-be would have been. One can imagine the shock this poor man experienced when his fiancée told him she was mysteriously pregnant. By that time, their intent to marry would have been known to both of their families and to the other villagers, and when this situation is viewed in the context of conservative village life, one can also imagine the volatility it would have generated.

Joseph must have spent much time agonizing over what to do now that Mary was pregnant, and not by him. Young men before and after his time have faced similar situations, and some have abandoned or even murdered their fiancées. It says a great deal about Joseph's character that he planned to leave her in a way that would not embarrass or disgrace her.

Here God intervened. An angel appeared to Joseph in a dream and told him, "Fear not to take unto thee Mary thy wife: for that which is conceived in her is of the Holy Ghost" (Matt. 1:20). Joseph obeyed.

Some who have been sadly misguided by the Roman Church claim that Mary was immaculate or sinless. This is a blatant contradiction of the Bible, which says, "All have sinned, and come short of the glory of God" (Rom. 3:23). God never proclaimed that Mary was immaculate. She was chosen by God as fitting for a role that she humbly accepted. If she had been sinless, then Jesus had come to save the world minus one person. "All have sinned" includes Mary. Only Jesus is without sin (see 1 Peter 2:22). Mary said, "My spirit hath rejoiced in God my Saviour" (Luke 1:47). A savior is needed by sinners, not by sinless ones. Romans 3:10 says, "There is none righteous, no, not one."

The Catholic Church claims that Joseph did not have a sexual relationship with Mary; thus, the theory of a "virgin Mary." This unnecessary, baseless attribution is used by the church to promote her sainthood and many other related deceptions. Matthew is plain on this matter when he writes that Joseph was not intimate with Mary *until* she gave birth to her firstborn son (Matt. 1:24). Joseph had four sons in that marriage, as well as daughters.

According to the Catholic Church, Mary died at the age of fifty-nine in the year AD 48. In that case, she would have been born around 12 BC. This cannot be accurate because Jesus Himself was born on an unknown date between 6 BC and 4 BC, since historians have recorded the death of Herod the Great as occurring in 6 BC. Some believe that Mary died in Jerusalem, but others believe she died in the city of Ephesus, which is in present day Turkey. Despite the differences of opinion, many people visit a place in Jerusalem that is supposed to be the tomb of Mary.

In fact, the theory of the Assumption of Mary is not very old. This presumption was authorized as authentic by Pope Pius XII on November 1, 1950. It took 1,900 years for the church to confirm her Assumption. Until then, this theory repeatedly cropped up and was suppressed. Thus, in the last century, Marian worship found a permanent place in the Catholic liturgy, and the Assumption of the Blessed Virgin Mary is celebrated on the fifteenth of August.

After the ascension of Jesus, the apostles obeyed Jesus' command and remained in Jerusalem. They were gathered together in an upper room, and that is the last biblical record of Mary (see Acts 1:14). The Catholic Church tried to find some further scriptural reference to Mary and focused their attention on the woman found in the twelfth chapter of the book of Revelation. This is, however, a clear case of mistaken identity.

Chapter 3

Mistaken Identity

—◦◦◦—

"And there appeared a great wonder in heaven; a woman clothed with the sun, and the moon under her feet, and upon her head a crown of twelve stars" (Rev. 12:1).

People like to choose verses and symbols of the Bible to fit their own agenda, but it is sad to hear them take biblical issues out of context to try to prove their point. The inspired Word of God is not a thing to take lightly. No one is allowed to add to or take away from what is recorded in the scriptures (see Rev. 22:18, 19). Misinterpretations of the scriptures have done irreparable damage to the cause of God by distorting plain truth to make people feel better about sin. Below are common fallacies promoted by those who do not know what the Bible really teaches:

- You can eat anything.
- It is OK to drink a little alcohol.
- The Lord's Day is Sunday.
- There is no harm in baptizing by sprinkling a little water on the head.
- The dead are in heaven.

- Sinners are burning in an everlasting hell.
- Saints can represent us before God.
- By offering a requiem mass, we can help our dear ones in purgatory to go to heaven.
- Praying the same prayer many times pleases God.

Catholics argue that since the good go to heaven and the wicked go to hell after death, there must be a place between heaven and hell for those who were not terribly good and not terribly bad; hence, the concept of purgatory. In response to the question of why purgatory is not found in the Bible, Catholics quickly reply that even words like "trinity" and "Bible" are also not found in the Bible. This is just a weak attempt to justify the invention of purgatory. They believe there is a difference between those who have sinned a lot and those who have sinned a little, so they say that only those who have sinned a lot are in hell. Therefore, purgatory exists to perfect for heaven those who have only sinned a little.

One spring Monday I entered a Catholic Church to rest my feet while on my way to the town library. The day before had been Palm Sunday, and a few devotees were engaged in silent prayer before the statue of Mary. As I left I picked up a church bulletin, and on the second page was a list of upcoming events, baptisms, and mass intentions. The first five masses on Palm Sunday were offered for various people, whose names were given. The last mass was for the parishioners. Monday morning's mass was for the souls in purgatory.

All of us have loved ones who have died who were not the best of saints or the worst of sinners, and Catholics believe that mass for these moderately wicked individuals will eventually promote them to heaven. This concept took root in the church during the Middle Ages and is just as strong today. But do sinners have to suffer in a particular location after their death in order to be saved? No. After death, the dead know nothing (see Eccles. 9:5; Ps. 146:4). Dead people do not experience pain or pleasure. Spiritual matters must be settled in this life; sinners do not suffer for their sins after death. Christ suffered for our sins, and if anyone teaches that sinners have to suffer to be saved, he belittles Christ's payment for sin by His suffering (see Rom. 5:8; Isa. 53:5; 1 John 2:2). If sinners were saved by suffering after death, they wouldn't need a Redeemer.

"The advancing centuries witnessed a constant increase of error in the doctrines put forth from Rome. Even before the establishment of the papacy the teachings of heathen philosophers had received attention and exerted an influence in the church. Many who professed conversion still clung to the tenets of their pagan philosophy, and not only continued its study themselves, but urged it upon others as a means of extending their influence among the heathen. Serious errors were thus introduced into the Christian faith. Prominent among these was the belief in man's natural immortality and his consciousness in death. This doctrine laid the foundation upon which Rome established the invocation of saints and the adoration of the Virgin Mary. From this sprang also the heresy of eternal torment for the finally impenitent, which was early incorporated into the papal faith.

"Then the way was prepared for the introduction of still another invention of paganism, which Rome named purgatory, and employed to terrify credulous and superstitious multitudes. By this heresy is affirmed the existence of a place of torment, in which the souls of such as have not merited eternal damnation are to suffer punishment for their sins, and from which, when freed from impurity, they are admitted to heaven" (*The Great Controversy*, p. 58, 59).

Because the dead do not know anything, the woman spoken of in the twelfth chapter of Revelation is not Mary.

This symbolic figure has been sadly misunderstood by both Catholics and Orthodox believers, and this woman will be discussed in detail after a review of the background of this prophetic book.

The apostle John wrote the book of Revelation based on a supernatural vision he received from God. In the very first sentence of this book, John records that this is "the Revelation of Jesus Christ, which God gave unto him, to shew unto his servants things which must shortly come to pass" (Rev. 1:1). This vision was a direct message from God to the church. It contains letters to seven geographical churches that existed at that time, but it is also understood that those churches represent seven periods of the church from apostolic time to the last days. We are living now in the Laodicean church period, which is evident in the wretched, pitiful, poor, blind, and naked spiritual condition of believers.

After the messages to the seven churches, John describes the throne room in heaven. Then he sees the Lamb (Jesus) coming to open a specific scroll, breaking its seven seals and delivering its messages one after the other. Thereafter, he talks about seven trumpets which are blown by seven angels in succession. Each time a trumpet is sounded, a great event follows. In the tenth chapter, after the sixth trumpet is sounded, a small book is mentioned. The great disappointment depicted by this small book took place in 1844. The eleventh chapter talks about two witnesses, which represent the Old and New Testaments or the Bible itself. This chapter tells of the suppression of the Bible during a certain period of time. In the twelfth chapter we read about a woman, who is misunderstood by the Roman Church to be Mary. There were no records of Mary after the first chapter of the book of Acts, and this lack of mention was a disadvantage to those who were determined to establish Mary's sainthood. The woman in the twelfth chapter of the book of Revelation conveniently filled the vacuum.

Since the time man fell in the Garden of Eden, there has been a fierce battle raging between Satan and the descendants of Adam. Among the human nations that came from the first couple, there have always been two distinct classes. One class obeyed God and remained faithful to Him no matter what. The other class rebelled and disobeyed God.

The faithful ones were God's people, and they were named later as Christ's church. Satan was not worried about those nominal "Christians" who were already on his side, but he was determined to harm Christ's church. He did everything he could to attack Christ and then killed the sin-bearing Savior on the cross. But the grave could not hold Christ forever and He arose victorious. Satan was defeated. When Jesus ascended to heaven and left behind His church on earth, Satan focused his attention on Christ's followers— the church. Attacking the apple of Jesus' eye is the best way Satan can hurt Him. The remnant church of God, the segment of the faithful who remained loyal throughout earth's history despite threats to their lives, is represented by the woman in Revelation chapter twelve.

This woman is portrayed as clothed with the sun and with the moon under her feet. Here the sun represents God's glory as revealed in the gospel, which is the beauty of the church. We know the moon does not have any light radiating from it since it is not a source of light. So why is this woman standing on the moon? The moon reflects the light of the sun. Here the moon represents the sacrificial system that points forward to a Redeemer who would come at the appointed time. This Redeemer was represented by an animal, usually a lamb, that was sacrificed by sinners for their sins. This symbolic system was fulfilled by the life and death of Jesus Christ. Therefore, the attachment of the symbols of sun and the moon was appropriate to the woman, the church. The crown of twelve stars worn by the woman represents the twelve apostles.

The twelfth chapter of Revelation succinctly tells the history of the church, covering a time span of about 1,800 years from the birth of Jesus to the end of the time of affliction suffered by the church, as well as unknown times in the past when the battle in heaven took place. Throughout the Bible a pure woman always represents the true church, while an impure woman represents a false church.

In John's vision the woman adorned with the sun, moon, and stars is the true church, who went into hiding for 1,260 years during the Dark Ages because of the atrocities carried out by the false church. The boy child, Jesus, was born to the loyal church of God in a general sense rather than to Mary individually. Through Herod the Great, Satan attempted to destroy the newborn infant and is depicted as the red dragon with seven heads and ten horns. He is identified by name in verse nine: "And the great dragon was cast out, that old serpent, called the Devil, and Satan, which deceiveth the whole world" (see also Rev. 20:2). Satan and his rebellious angels were defeated by Michael (Jesus) and His angels, and the evil ones were expelled from heaven. Satan deceived and took with him one-third of the heavenly host of angels (see Rev. 12:4).

The two contrasting women in Revelation, one pure and one impure, are symbolic of those who are loyal to God and those who have gone astray. The true church is referred to as the bride and the Lamb's wife, whereas the false church is depicted as an adulterous woman and a whore. These names illustrate the character of the two churches.

It was not the Bible writers who used these conflicting allegories, but it was God Himself. He says, "I likened the daughter of Zion to a comely and delicate woman" (Jeremiah 6:2), and "For I am jealous over you with godly jealousy: for I have espoused you to one husband, that I may present you as a chaste virgin to Christ" (2 Cor. 11:2).

God always cared for His people, and He made important covenants with them. What undergirded these covenants was fidelity; therefore, the bond between God and His people was like a marital relationship. God's people were like a bride to Him—cherished, cared for, and protected by Him. It broke God's heart to see His people following after pagan gods that are Satan's hoaxes, and their abandonment of Him and going after other gods is compared to adultery. Throughout the Bible a church, a body of believers, is symbolized by a woman. It is only a symbol, and love built on mutual trust is what God expects of His people.

In general God's people were faithful to Him, but we find clear evidence in Scripture that there were times when the majority of the Israelite nation worshipped other gods. The body of believers now is divided on doctrines, principles, rituals, and opinions. Both sides say they are the church of God, but one side does not know that they have been rejected for their disobedience, arrogance, and self-dependence. The emergence of a false church was foretold by the prophet Daniel, and it fulfills the prophecy to the letter.

1. It speaks words against the Most High. Daniel was shown a religious-political power emerging under the pretext of being God's church. This power assumed titles belonging only to God and is currently called Most Holy Father, Representative of God, and Father of the church.

2. It oppresses the holy ones of the Most High. As this entity came to the forefront in the year AD 538, the faithful ones of God did not accept him as their head.

This made a clear division among the Christians. The dissenters were ruthlessly persecuted and thousands were put to death. "Christians" persecuted Christians.

3. It changes times and laws. By now you may be able guess who this power is. It is the papacy. The papacy did change times and laws. The commandments were changed at the discretion of the leaders of the Catholic Church, and they boldly acknowledge it. The second commandment, which prohibited idol worship, was discarded. The fourth commandment, which required observance of the seventh-day Sabbath, was changed. The tenth commandment was split in two to compensate for the loss of the second.

4. It persecuted the saints of God for 1,260 years, which is the most significant sign of this power.

We will go into details later regarding the above characteristics of the leadership of the false church, but this discussion has been sufficient to discern that there are two basic churches existing in the world today. There may be thousands of churches by different names, but there are two churches by their characteristics. The true church has the commandments of God and the testimony of Jesus. The false church adheres to their own commandments, which have been rendered invalid by unauthorized tampering by humans. Even though those churches have denominational names to identify them separately, they all stand under one umbrella by keeping as holy the first day of the week, Sunday. For further information on this topic, read the book *National Sunday Law.*

The church bowed to tradition and culture in Rome where Sunday was a pagan worship day. By accepting this first day of the week as the Sabbath day, the church could welcome pagans into the faith with less persuasion. Thus Christendom exhibited two divided groups. While the majority embraced the first day as the Sabbath, the minority remained true to God's command and kept the seventh day holy.

This corrupt church system is portrayed in the Bible as great Babylon or a whore. A whore welcomes into intimate relationship men who are not her husband. The husband or head of the church is God, but this corrupt church allowed pagans to enter the church and wooed kings and rulers of nations. She arrogantly cultivated military force in place of God-fearing piety. God, who longed to dwell with His people, moved out of this abominable hoax of a church.

As you can see, attempting to find a niche for Mary in the book of Revelation is a futile effort. This book and the gospels were written to highlight Jesus and His ministry. None of the other characters were as important. Mary was a secondary character, as were the rest of them. The gospel writers were not concerned about the relationship of the Lord to any one person, not because they purposely ignored them, but because Jesus always outshone everyone else. Stars are not visible in the sky when the sun is shining in full glory.

Joseph is mentioned in the gospels of Luke and Matthew. When Jesus was twelve years old, Joseph and Mary were shocked to find that Jesus was not with them as they were returning home from the temple in Jerusalem. They would have been journeying in the midst of a milling crowd, and in the hustle and bustle, they thought Jesus was somewhere in the crowd. When they noticed that Jesus was not with them, they immediately rushed back to Jerusalem. If just the three of them had been making this trip, Jesus' absence would have been noticed much sooner. It is very likely that Jesus' siblings and their neighbors were traveling with them as well. This annual journey to the temple covered a distance of more than sixty miles, so by the time Mary and Joseph discovered that Jesus was not with them, they had already traveled for an entire day (see Luke 2:44).

Joseph was not the biological father of Jesus, but he was descended from the line of Abraham and David. The faithful ones of the descendants of Adam were to go forth generation to generation in their faithful journey. A genealogical line was to proceed uninterrupted with hallmarks such as Abraham, Isaac, Jacob, and David. The gospel of Matthew shows this genealogy from Abraham to David, David to Babylonian exile, and from exile to the Messiah.

During Jesus' public ministry, the people who knew Him were astonished when He came back to His hometown doing and saying noble and majestic things. They whispered among themselves, "Is not this the carpenter's son?" (Matt. 13:55). The Greek word translated as "carpenter" is *tektōn,* which referred to anyone who worked with wood. The people were angry and resented it that this lad from their village acted like He was better than they were. Their statement was sarcastic, "Is not his mother called Mary? And his brethren, James, and Joses, and Simon, and Judas?" (verse 55). Mark says that Jesus had sisters as well (see Mark 6:3).

Were they all Mary's children? We do not know for sure. Some say they were the children of Joseph's previous marriage, and some say they were Mary's children. We simply do not know. Poor families often have more children than well-to-do families.

We do know that Joseph was the earthly father of Jesus, the husband of Mary, and a hard-working poor man. In order to gather related facts of Joseph, though, one must search apocryphal writings. The dependability and trustworthiness of those documents cannot be ascertained because they have been left out of the Bible. It is believed that Joseph was born in Bethlehem, and it is traditionally accepted that he died in Nazareth in the year AD 18. The gospel writer Mark makes no mention of Joseph, and Paul, who wrote many epistles, does not refer to Joseph or Mary anywhere in his writings. Joseph did his part and faded away into obscurity.

After the birth of Jesus, the three of them remained in Bethlehem for a short while. They weren't in a hurry to begin the arduous journey back to Nazareth with an infant.

Sometime later, Herod became angry that the wise men had not returned to tell him the location of the newborn king. An angel had instructed them not to go back to Herod, but to return home another way. Angels appointed by God to take care of the infant Jesus were busy making sure that He was safe. An angel appeared to Joseph in a dream and told him to flee to Egypt, and the new parents escaped with the child and remained in Egypt until they heard that Herod the Great had died. They returned to Judea only to learn that Herod's son Archelaus was now the ruler of Judea. Deeming it unsafe to live in Judea, they moved to Nazareth in Galilee where Jesus lived a quiet life until the day He went to the river Jordan to be baptized by His cousin John.

It is interesting to note that only three family members fled to Egypt. "And when they [the wise men] were departed, behold, the angel of the Lord appeareth to Joseph in a dream, saying, Arise, and take the young child and his mother, and flee into Egypt, and be thou there until I bring thee word: for Herod will seek the young child to destroy him" (Matt. 2:13). It appears that the couple had only one child at that time. About thirty years later, however, during Jesus' public ministry, He had four brothers and at least two sisters. Two gospel writers plainly write that Jesus had brothers and sisters as they record the sarcastic comments of those who knew this family well. In the book of Acts, the brothers of Jesus are briefly mentioned (see Acts 1:14).

The Jewish nation was waiting for their Messiah, a hero who would come to free them from Roman bondage. There had been many courageous young patriots from time to time who led revolutions against Roman rule. However, all of these revolutions were crushed by the Roman rulers, who were military masterminds. Rome had administrative power as well as the manpower in the form of well-trained troops. Any man who was bold enough to stand against the oppressors was backed by many others who risked losing their lives.

The Jews watched this charismatic youth who had the courage to stand for his views. His miracles gave them hope, but when they learned that He talked about a kingdom of grace instead of a kingdom of power, they moved on. The age-old hope of a conquering king kept burning in their hearts. A king would not only transform them into a sovereign nation, but also relieve them from the heavy taxes that had been imposed on them. This hope was held even by Mary.

"Yet Mary did not understand Christ's mission. Simeon had prophesied of Him as a light to lighten the Gentiles, as well as a glory to Israel. Thus the angels had announced the Saviour's birth as tidings of joy to all peoples. God was seeking to correct the narrow, Jewish conception of the Messiah's work. He desired men to behold Him, not merely as the deliverer of Israel, but as the Redeemer of the world. But many years must pass before even the mother of Jesus would understand His mission" (*The Desire of Ages*, p. 56).

The gospel writers record that Jesus talked about His heavenly Father many times, but they do not record that He mentioned Joseph at all. It was true that Joseph protected and looked after Jesus, but after his role in Jesus' life was done, it was over.

The apostles' eloquent sermons and lengthy epistles during the first century never referred to Mary or Joseph; their focus was on Jesus. They had no Mary or Joseph veneration among them because they knew the truth about the state of the dead. I have seen many icons and statues of Joseph that depict him as an old man. Imagine Mary living with a man who resembled her father or grandfather. This is a well-thought-out scheme of the Catholic Church to portray Joseph as a weak, elderly man who wouldn't have any interest in his virgin wife. Joseph was not an old man. He labored in a carpenter shop to provide for his family. He walked with Mary yearly from Nazareth to Jerusalem since it was obligatory for all able-bodied and healthy males to attend the temple ceremonies on high days. He rushed to Egypt with Mary to save the life of the Child Jesus; he was fit for long-distance trips.

Mary faithfully carried out her role as Jesus' mother as expected by God. "The child Jesus did not receive instruction in the synagogue schools. His mother was His first human teacher. From her lips and from the scrolls of prophets, He learned of heavenly things. The very words which He Himself had spoken to Moses for Israel He was now taught at His mother's knee. As He advanced from childhood to youth, He did not seek the schools of the rabbis. He needed not the education to be obtained from such sources; for God was His instructor" (*The Desire of Ages*, p. 70).

Those who are obsessed with Mary will apply to this poor woman every possible Bible verse containing the word "woman" and call any shadow or reflection her apparition. Such people are intoxicated with the deceptive teachings of Babylon. Multiple prophecies had been given about the birth, birthplace, ministry, suffering, sacrificial death, and ascension of Jesus, but neither Mary nor Joseph were named in prophecies. The only exception is in the Book of Mormon:

"And he shall be called Jesus Christ, the Son of God, the Father of heaven and earth, the Creator of all things from the beginning; and his mother shall be called Mary" (Mosiah 3:8). Those who gave Mary undeserved promotions were keen on finding some scriptural backing for these accolades. That is why they have erroneously applied nearly every biblical occurrence of the word "woman" to Mary.

Apparitions are supposed to be appearances by dead people. In other words they are visible "ghosts." Among the apparitions recorded and recognized by the Catholic Church, we find Mary, Jesus, angels, and some other saints. However, Jesus is alive. He is not dead and would not appear as an apparition. He promised to come again physically, which will happen at His second coming. If anyone says that He has already appeared somewhere before and every eye has not seen Him, that statement goes against the Bible—against what Jesus said (see Matt. 24:23). The Bible clearly teaches that the dead have turned to dust and that their thoughts are no more (see Gen. 3:19; Eccles. 9:5). The apparition that appeared to King Saul was not the prophet Samuel. It was a mere impersonation performed by the devil, who has insisted throughout the ages that humans continue to exist beyond death with their complete memories and other capabilities.

"The doctrine of man's consciousness in death, especially the belief that spirits of the dead return to minister to the living, has prepared the way for modern spiritualism. If the dead are admitted to the presence of God and holy angels, and privileged with knowledge far exceeding what they before possessed, why should they not return to the earth to enlighten and instruct the living? If, as taught by popular theologians, spirits of the dead are hovering about their friends on earth, why should they not be permitted to communicate with them, to warn them against evil, or to comfort them in sorrow? How can those who believe in man's consciousness in death reject what comes to them as divine light communicated from glorified spirits? Here is a channel regarded as sacred, through which Satan works for the accomplishment of his purposes. The fallen angels who do his bidding appear as messengers from the spirit world. While professing to bring the living into communication with the dead, the prince of evil exercises his bewitching influence upon their minds.

"He has power to bring before men the appearance of their departed friends. The counterfeit is perfect; the familiar look, the words, the tone, are reproduced with marvelous distinctness. Many are comforted with the assurance that their loved ones are enjoying the bliss of heaven, and without suspicion of danger, they give ear 'to seducing spirits and doctrines of devils.'

"When they have been led to believe that the dead actually return to communicate with them, Satan causes those to appear who went into the grave unprepared. They claim to be happy in heaven and even to occupy exalted positions there, and thus the error is widely taught that no difference is made between the righteous and the wicked. The pretended visitants from the world of spirits sometimes utter cautions and warnings which prove to be correct. Then, as confidence is gained, they present doctrines that directly undermine faith in the Scriptures. With an appearance of deep interest in the well-being of their friends on earth, they insinuate the most dangerous errors. The fact that they state some truths, and are able at times to foretell future events, gives to their statements an appearance of reliability; and their false teachings are accepted by the multitudes as readily, and believed as implicitly, as if they were the most sacred truths of the Bible. The law of God is set aside, the Spirit of grace despised, the blood of the covenant counted an unholy thing. The spirits deny the deity of Christ and place even the Creator on a level with themselves. Thus under a new disguise the great rebel still carries on his warfare against God, begun in heaven and for nearly six thousand years continued upon the earth....

"...Many will be ensnared through the belief that spiritualism is a merely human imposture; when brought face to face with manifestations which they cannot but regard as supernatural, they will be deceived, and will be led to accept them as the great power of God" (*The Great Controversy*, pp. 551–553).

The devil can appear in the form of a person who has died, and it is not hard for him to do it through the powers with which he was vested before the fall. Demons lost angelic privileges but retain much power. They have led humans to destruction through the lie that their dead loved ones are living in hell, heaven, or purgatory. This belief has caused many to become involved in subtle spiritualistic rituals. They firmly believe that their loved ones, in most cases, are in heaven. Guidance by clergy has become an effective support to the devilish deception. They say, and even advertise in newspapers, that the dear one who departed lately is "in the sweet arms of Jesus." Jesus does not take each dead person in His arms to rock them and sing lullabies. This phrase, "in the arms of Jesus," has become a common phrase of consolation that has no validity.

What then is Jesus doing in heaven? He has a great responsibility to fulfill, and He is faithfully engaged in it right now. This phase in the plan of salvation that He is performing now is that of High Priest in the heavenly sanctuary. The earthly sanctuary that Moses was instructed to build was to be patterned after the one that is in heaven (see Acts 7:44).

"After His ascension, our Saviour was to begin His work

as our High Priest. Says Paul, 'Christ is not entered into the holy places made with hands, which are the figures of the true; but into heaven itself, now to appear in the presence of God for us.' Hebrews 9:24. As Christ's ministration was to consist of two great divisions, each occupying a period of time and having a distinctive place in the heavenly sanctuary, so typical ministration consisted of two divisions, the daily and the yearly service, and to each a department of the tabernacle was devoted.

"As Christ at His ascension appeared in the presence of God to plead His blood in behalf of penitent believers, so the priest in the daily ministration sprinkled the blood of the sacrifice in the holy place in the sinner's behalf" (*Patriarchs and Prophets*, p. 357).

The sanctuary service, as recorded in the Old Testament, has enormous significance in the plan of salvation. God asked Moses to build a portable sanctuary while the Israelites were on their way to the Promised Land from Egypt. This large, meticulously built tent had two sections: the holy place and the Most Holy Place. The high priest intervened daily for sinners by sprinkling the blood of sacrificed animals on the curtain that separated the Most Holy Place from the holy place. The high priest ministered in this way throughout the year, except on one day. On the Day of Atonement, he entered the Most Holy Place after the prescribed preparation to conduct the annual service that cleansed the sanctuary of the accumulated sins. This was a day that was taken very seriously by the whole Israelite encampment for God had warned that anyone who was not free from sin would be cut off on that day. The sanctuary service system instituted in the wilderness has a vital connection to the plan of salvation entrusted to Jesus Christ, and He is now engaged in the last portion of it.

After Jesus fulfilled the role of the sacrificial Lamb, which made salvation of sinners possible, He began His role in the last part of the plan of salvation upon His arrival in heaven. He is now pleading for sinners as our High Priest in the sanctuary of heaven. When His responsibilities in the holy place were completed, He entered the Most Holy Place. This sequence of events is easily understood by reading chapters in the Old Testament that describe the sanctuary services.

Jesus entered the Most Holy Place in the heavenly sanctuary on October 22, 1844. You may wonder how we know the exact date. There are several prophecies in the Bible that contribute to an understanding of this date, and the longest time prophecy is found in the book of Daniel. "And he said unto me, Unto two thousand and three hundred days; then shall the sanctuary be cleansed" (Dan. 8:14).

Are you puzzled? Don't worry; even Daniel was, and the angel Gabriel was sent to explain the vision to the prophet. Gabriel said, "Understand, O son of man: for at the time of the end shall be the vision" (Dan. 8:17). The angel's explanation was not easy for Daniel to comprehend even though he was known for his great intelligence. "I was astonished at the vision, but none understood it," he said (verse 27). When we are given a riddle or puzzle to figure out or a prophecy related to a time period, we naturally think of its starting point. The angel did give Daniel that vital clue, but before we get to that point there is something we should understand: A day in prophecy equals a year (see Num. 14:34; Ezek. 4:6). In addition to the 2,300-day prophecy given in the eighth chapter of Daniel, another prophecy of seventy weeks, or 490 days, is given in the ninth chapter.

According to Daniel 9:24, the seventy-week time period was given exclusively for Daniel's people, the Jews, to:

1. "finish the transgression,"
2. "make an end of sins,"
3. "make reconciliation for iniquity,"
4. "bring in everlasting righteousness,"
5. "seal up the vision and prophecy," and
6. "anoint the most Holy."

These are the six items on the agenda to be carried out during this prophetic time of seventy weeks, which equals 490 literal years. "Know therefore and understand, that from the going forth of the commandment to restore and to build Jerusalem unto the Messiah the Prince shall be seven weeks, and threescore and two weeks" (Dan. 9:25).

There was a reason for these sixty-nine weeks' time to be given as seven weeks plus sixty-two weeks. As we read the biblical record of the prophecy's fulfillment, it took seven prophetic weeks, or forty-nine literal years, to rebuild the walls around the city of Jerusalem. Daniel kept thinking and searching and in the end found some hint in the book of Jeremiah that said Jerusalem would remain desolate for seventy years. As God had forewarned, Jerusalem underwent enemy attack because of the unfaithfulness of its people. The Babylonians attacked, looted, and burned the city. Many Israelites, including Daniel, were taken away as prisoners.

In order to understand these mysterious prophetic matters, Daniel continued in prayer and supplication. He began by saying, "O Lord, the great and dreadful God, keeping the covenant and mercy to them that love him, and to them that keep his commandments" (Dan. 9:4). In the above statement, we see with whom God is keeping His gracious covenant: those who love Him and keep His commandments. Shouldn't this fact open the eyes of anyone who ignores the commandments of God?

Daniel's prayer was answered. The angel Gabriel came back to explain the seventy week-time period. This we find to be the first segment of the 2,300 year period. "Seventy weeks are determined upon thy people and upon thy holy city" (Dan. 9:24). Because a day in prophecy stands for a year in our time, the seventy prophetic weeks (490 prophetic days) equal 490 literal years. The obstinate, hard-hearted Israelites were given 490 years to prove themselves as a nation worthy of God's blessings and to be light bearers to the world.

The starting point of this time period would be the year in which the Persian king issued a decree to restore and rebuild Jerusalem. "Know therefore and understand, that from the going forth of the commandment to restore and to build Jerusalem unto the Messiah the Prince shall be seven weeks, and threescore and two weeks" (Dan. 9:25). This foreign king who ruled over the Israelites became a benevolent helper to God's people and allowed them to go and rebuild Jerusalem. With king's financial assistance, some of the Jews returned to Jerusalem to begin the work of restoration in 457 BC. That was the year the prophetic time period began. The total time period of seventy weeks, or 490 literal years, was divided by the angel into three segments as seven weeks, sixty-two weeks, and one week.

During the first segment of seven weeks, or forty-nine literal years, the walls around the city of Jerusalem were built under Nehemiah's management.

The next segment of sixty-two weeks, or 434 literal years, was intended for the nation to prepare to welcome the Messiah. But they didn't, and this time segment ended in AD 27.

The last segment of one week, or 7 literal years, began in AD 27 when the Messiah, the Anointed One, began His public ministry by being baptized in the river Jordan. "And he shall confirm the covenant with many for one week: and in the midst of the week he shall cause the sacrifice and the oblation to cease" (Dan. 9:27). This meticulously accurate prophecy was given to Daniel 560 years before the birth of Christ. The Messiah was cut off in the middle of the week, three and a half years after He began his public ministry— He was crucified in AD 31. Three and half years later, the seventy-year grace period for God's chosen nation ended in AD 34, with the merciless stoning of Stephen, the first Christian martyr. God's chosen nation had been given seventy prophetic weeks—490 literal years—to make matters right, but instead they killed the Messiah and His followers. At the end of this 490-year period, the message of salvation went out to the Gentiles. This is when apostles began to spread out across Gentile territories and converted multitudes. This 490-year period is the first part of the great time prophecy of 2,300 days/years. The decree issued by the Persian king Artaxerxes in 457 BC set in motion the historical events that concluded with the cold-blooded slaughter of Stephen in AD 34.

Notice that we are still engaged in the quest to learn what Jesus is doing in heaven presently. As mentioned before, He entered the heavenly sanctuary as the High Priest when He ascended to heaven. The heavenly sanctuary has two sections just as the earthly sanctuary did. The priestly duties in the first section, called the Holy Place, ended in the year 1844, and this will be clear in our further study of the 2,300-year period.

Once again, as we look at the fourteenth verse of Daniel 8, we consider the cleansing of the sanctuary. The earthly sanctuary was cleansed annually on the tenth day of the seventh month according to the Hebrew calendar. Now as we count down 2,300 years from 457 BC, we end up in AD 1843. Because there is no zero year—AD 1 came after 1 BC—we move the date to AD 1844. By this time there was not an earthly sanctuary. The Temple in Jerusalem was destroyed in AD 70, and only a massive wall of enormous stones was left behind. Yet according to the prophecy, a sanctuary had to be cleansed in AD 1844. In the absence of a tabernacle or sanctuary on the earth, some guessed that it might be the church. However, the only text supporting this view is Psalms chapter 114, verses one and two, which says that Judah became God's sanctuary. This cannot be valid as the tribe of Judah is only a part of the church. Therefore, it is appropriate in every sense to accept the idea that the sanctuary referred in Daniel 8:14 is the original one in heaven, which was the pattern by which the tabernacle in the desert was built.

Excited preachers such as William Miller preached day and night prior to and during the year 1844, emphatically saying that the world would end on October 22, 1844. They wholeheartedly believed that the sanctuary mentioned in Daniel 8:14 was the earth. They had to rethink that belief when October 22 brought an end to nothing except their preaching.

Yet the prophecy *was* fulfilled on that day, and further study of the Scriptures afterward affirmed that the fulfillment took place in heaven. Just as the earthly high priest entered the Most Holy Place once a year, on the tenth day of the seventh month of the Hebrew calendar, that very same day and date, Jesus entered the heavenly Most High Place to begin the final phase of His service before the throne of God. The Day of Atonement on earth was a decisive, critical day for the Israelites in the camp around the earthly sanctuary, and now it a decisive time for us living on this earth during the time of the judgment in heaven.

Many churches teach about the judgment day in different tones and make us feel that this day is the end of the world. It may be so in one sense, but judgment is being carried out in heaven now. This is an elaborate process that cannot be expedited for any reason because each person's case is being considered to determine eternal consequences. With the clear knowledge that you and I will soon be judged, if we have not been already, how careful we ought to be.

We ventured into the above discussion trying to answer the question: What is Jesus doing in heaven? Based on the Scripture, He is engaged in the judgment process in heaven. That is His service in God's agenda right now. Therefore, let us not fool ourselves that He is keeping our departed dead ones in his alms. Departed dead ones are in the dust, and Jesus is deciding on their eternity during the judgment. When Jesus returns in the clouds of glory, He will gather the saved and take them to heaven.

That's why it is so important for people to know the truth about Marian worship. Jesus is judging the world, and those who are not following the truth of the Bible will have to answer for their beliefs before the Lord.

One belief that surrounds Marian worship is the idea of the immaculate conception. Thomas Aquinas was foremost among many who promoted Marian worship in the Catholic Church, but he and many early Catholic theologians could not agree on the idea of the immaculate conception. Finally they determined that Mary was born without the original sin, thus the idea of the immaculate conception.

Also, take into consideration the belief in Marian sightings. No pope, cardinal, bishop, or priest has been lucky enough to see Mary appearing to them, but many children or common people claim to have seen her. Satan knows who to deceive and how to deceive. Educated people verify matters in ways that common people don't. Some people in my country tell stories of a woman appearing to men who travel alone at night in rural roads. They say that it is a she-devil named Mohini. Similar episodes are heard from India too. I also find it interesting that Mary has only appeared to Catholics who recognize her without any hesitation. How come no Methodist, Baptist, or Seventh-day Adventist has been lucky enough to see an apparition of Mary? That is because the devil knows who to trick to keep his deception alive, and those who are grounded in the truth will not fall for his lies.

Chapter 4

Mary's Self-Esteem

—◦◦◦—

The world has been programmed to regard Mary as a stereotype. As we have discussed, she has been elevated to the level of God in regard to worship. The adoration and the veneration given to her surpass the same given to any other saint and even to God. The reason for this special treatment is because she is the mother of God's Son. This fact, when officially recognized in AD 431 at the Ephesian Council, caused the Marian cult to plant firm roots among many churches.

Jesus was before Mary. In fact, during His public ministry, Jesus once said that He was before Abraham, long before Mary was born. Also Jesus prayed, "O Father glorify thou me with thine own self with that glory which I had with thee before the world was" (John 17:5). The Catholic argument is that Mary is the mother of Jesus and Jesus is God, so Mary is the mother of God. This is the logic that they use to justify this doctrine.

Mary was chosen for her particular role because of her qualifying characteristics such as humility, truthfulness, and lovingkindness to everyone in her circle of influence—she

was loved by God and everyone who knew her. These positive characteristics do not mean she was perfect, but she was
willing to let God use her, and He did.

She, like so many other Bible characters, gave herself to
God for His service, with her strengths and weaknesses. Look
at Moses. He killed an Egyptian and fled the country, fearing
the king's wrath. He was a murderer. But God called him the
most humble man among men. The humility of Moses and
the fact that he surrendered to God endeared Moses to God.

Then look at Abraham. We find some shortcomings in
his life. Lying is a sin, and Abraham told a big lie to Pharaoh.
He said he was traveling with his sister, when Sarah was
really his wife. In spite of this mistake and others, God loved
Abraham for his faithfulness, and when Abraham was called
to sacrifice his own son, he didn't hesitate to offer his son to
the God he loved and trusted.

God loved David even though David had many wives
and arranged to kill Uriah in order to take his wife too. When
confronted with his sin, he repented like none did before. As
you read the psalms, in their genuine sincerity, you get a
glimpse of David's relationship with God. Poured out in each
psalm is devotion, fear, loneliness, embarrassment, victory,
success, disappointment, and failure. All these human emotions and more are painted in beautiful word pictures that
we can relate to. David wanted to build a temple for the Lord
since he was living in a comfortable fortified palace. But God
refused to accept his offer as David had "blood" on his hands.
In battle he was a fierce warrior who had killed countless en-
emies. So God gave the job of building the temple to David's
son Solomon. Yet God knew David's true nature. God said,
"I have found David the son of Jesse, a man after mine own
heart" (Acts 13:22), an honor not bestowed upon anyone else
in the Bible.

God the Father was pleased with Mary for her virtuous manners. She was selected to be the mother of His Son, the promised Messiah, and Mary fulfilled her duties as the mother of Jesus to the entire satisfaction of God. She accomplished her part in God's plan, just as Noah and others before her. Noah saved his wife, three sons and their wives, and a host of animals and birds from the deadly flood. Moses took the enslaved Israelites out of Egypt and led them to the Promised Land. And Daniel served as a faithful witness in a foreign land throughout his life.

Mary was a wonderful mother to Jesus. She sobbed at the cross for the loss of her Son, but she saw the empty tomb. She saw Him alive, and she witnessed His ascension to heaven. From the womb to the grave, she cared for Him. When He was little, she fed, bathed, dressed, instructed, and looked after Him. After His resurrection, her focus changed. She saw the risen Savior who conquered death for all humanity, including her. She saw Jesus ascend to heaven, and Mary joined with the other believers in praising God for His gift. She was no longer just a mother seeing her Son departing, but she was a believer who had a strong faith in Jesus as the risen King of the universe.

After the four Gospels and in the first chapter of Acts, we do not hear about Mary. However, there is one slight mention of the mother of Jesus in the book of Galatians: "But when the fulness of the time was come, God sent forth his Son, made of a woman" (Gal. 4:4). Paul may have met Mary, but we do not know for sure. What we do know is that none of the disciples or apostles seemed to pay extra attention to the mother of their Master as seen in the silence as to her life and ministry in the early church after Jesus' ascension. Sure, she was with the disciples, and she was regarded as one of the believers, but we do not witness any special interest given to her in the New Testament church. Of course, this attitude turned upside down in a couple of centuries after Jesus' ascension.

Mary knew who she was and her place in the growing church. There is no evidence that Mary took a leadership role in the early church. She had already fulfilled God's role for her by caring for Jesus from birth to death and resurrection. That was the assignment given to her by God. And so, this dignified woman quietly lived the rest of her life for her risen Savior, her Son, with her self-esteem in tact but not overly inflated.

Chapter 5

Where Are the Dead?

———⟨⟨⟨⟩⟩⟩———

Linked with Marian worship is the issue of the state of the dead. The Bible clearly tells us that a few individuals went to heaven without experiencing death. Enoch was the first recorded person to be taken alive to heaven according to the record of Moses (Gen. 5:24). As for the qualification he had for this unusual privilege, we read that he walked with God.

Then we find the heaven bound journey of the prophet Elijah. Elijah clashed with King Ahab, the ruler of the region who had turned away from God to worship a pagan god named Baal because of the evil influence of Jezebel, his wife. With his faith firmly planted in God, Elijah stood against the dominating Baal worship in the region and called for a showdown to prove that God was the one and only true God (1 Kings 17–19). Like Enoch, Elijah also was taken to heaven without seeing death (2 Kings 1, 2).

The third miraculous ascension documented in the Bible was that of Jesus, which His disciples and Mary witnessed. We also know that some righteous people were raised at the death of Jesus (Matt. 27:52, 53). These saints were taken to heaven as the first fruits of His redeeming work, but their mass ascension was not visible.

These ascensions are clearly documented in the Bible, but no such ascension of Mary is mentioned, although the Roman Catholic Church claims that she is in heaven. Marian worship is clearly a trap designed by Satan to turn people's attention away from God.

Up until the Pentecostal experience and the outpouring of the Holy Spirit that gave great doctrinal knowledge to the disciples of Jesus, they too were ignorant of many of the foundational truths of Christianity. This became evident with the news that Lazarus, who was a close friend of Jesus, was deathly ill. Jesus treated the urgent message with calmness, and he slowly began making his way to the village of Bethany where Lazarus lived with his two sisters, Martha and Mary. It was Mary who anointed the Lord with perfume and wiped his feet with her hair. She and her sister knew personally that Jesus could heal their brother.

Jesus did not panic over the news that his friend was going to die. He saw that Lazarus' sickness would lead to the glorification of God. He said: "This sickness is not unto death, but for the glory of God, that the Son of God might be glorified thereby" (John 11:4). "When he had heard therefore that he [Lazarus] was sick, he abode two days still in the same place where he was. Then after that saith he said to his disciples, Let us go into Judaea again" (verse 6, 7). It was quite a distance for them to travel to Bethany, and to make matters worse, they had to go through Jerusalem, where some Jews had recently attempted to stone Jesus, but Jesus was determined to go to Lazarus.

The disciples asked Him in surprise, "Master, the Jews of late sought to stone thee; and goest thou thither again?...

[Jesus] saith unto them, Our friend Lazarus sleepeth; but I go, that I may awake him out of sleep" (verses 8, 11). Jesus intentionally delayed the trip to teach them an important truth.

Now these men, not understanding what their Master meant, argued with Him: "Lord, if he sleep, he shall do well" (verse 12). Here the disciples argued with no clear understanding of the state of the dead. They walked with the Master, but they did not understand His teachings. This event reveals the great truth that death is compared to sleep. How beautiful it is to know that we are going to wake up after death. Lazarus was awakened by the voice of Jesus after three days in the grave.

Having lost immortality in the Garden of Eden, everyone is destined to die at some point and time. But God, with His limitless love for fallen humanity, gave everyone a second chance by accepting the wages of sin upon Himself. Jesus said that he had the power to lay down His life and take it back. We do not have the power to take back our life after death. But because of Jesus' sacrifice, the righteous have the assurance of waking up again. God adjusted and tamed death for our sake, but not for Satan and the wicked. He will not be given the chance to wake up after the final death that will befall him. When he dies, he will be gone forevermore, as will the wicked with him. They will be subject to eternal death.

Acquiring a strong and clear knowledge of the state of the dead will lead to an understanding of what the Catholic Church teaches. Satan misinterpreted the nature of death to his gain, and as long as people don't understand the real nature of the deceased, Satan will play on that misunderstanding.

God formed Adam and Eve out of dust, similar to a sculptor fashioning a statue. But God didn't stop there;

He breathed into Adam's nostrils the breath of life, and he became a living soul. A living soul has perfectly functioning systems in the body. People can do things, and think of things—they are conscious.

You and I are living souls or living beings. "The soul that sinneth, it shall die" (Ezek. 18:20). The person who sins and rejects God is destined to eternal death. This is what God said to Adam and Eve as a warning before the fall. There is no entity, which most people call the soul, that lives outside of the body. This idea that a soul exists separately from the body has led innumerable people to destruction. No souls are in heaven. It is not your soul, but your immortal body that will go to heaven on the day of resurrection.

Life is a gift of God to humanity—we are nothing but an activated mass of mud. Therefore, the moment we are separated from life, the breath of God, we are nothing but dust. Scientists have proved that all the elements found in the dust are found in the human body. King Solomon, the wisest man to ever live, wrote: "Then shall the dust return to the earth as it was: and the spirit [breath] shall return unto God who gave it" (Eccl. 12:7). The spirit that is given to us is the breath that belongs to God. Once separated from our body, the breath goes back to its Owner. "All the while my breath is in me, and the spirit of God is in my nostrils" (Job 27:3). We are conscious as long as our bodies retain the God-given spirit, the breath. David explains this phenomenon in Psalm 104: "Thou takest away their breath, they die, and return to their dust. Thou sendest forth thy spirit, they are created" (verses 29, 30).

These and other verses in Scripture present a clear picture of the state of the dead. Inspired writers of the Bible presented this truth throughout the Old and New Testament, and all their thoughts are in harmony.

Popular books, periodicals, and TV programs present stories of people who have experienced some type of near-death event where they go to heaven and see their dead relatives before coming back to this earth. Those who watch and read these fabrications instead of the Bible are dragged deeper in the labyrinth of deception. Those publications and programs are the most popular bestsellers. Those who find no thrill and fun in the truth, discover a trove of mind-tickling fantasies in these products, which are the deceptive work of the devil.

"For the time will come when they will not endure sound doctrine; but after their own lusts shall they heap to themselves teachers, having itching ears; and they shall turn away their ears from the truth, and shall be turned unto fables" (2 Tim. 4:3, 4).

Dead people know nothing. But living people have a functioning brain that is capable of thinking as well as retaining memory. Some elderly folks lose so much memory that they cannot recognize their spouses, children, and grandchildren because of worn out brain cells. If the memory loss of the living person can be so detrimental, there should be no doubt about the loss of memory of a dead person. The brain dies after the heart stops pumping blood and carrying oxygen to the brain cells. Once buried, the body gradually turns to dust, and still there is no more memory for that person. The cells that held the memory have turned to dust just as the rest of that person's body.

Let us listen to the inspired words of David and Solomon: "His breath goeth forth, he returneth to his earth; in that day his thoughts perish" (Ps. 146:4); "For the living know that they shall die: but the dead know not any thing" (Eccl. 9:5). This is the truth. The dead do not know anything, because they are sleeping in the ground. A living being can praise the Lord, but dead do not praise Him (Ps. 115:17).

The dead remain in the dust until the day comes to wake up at Christ's second coming. This is not a Halloween scene of zombies coming out of their graves. All who die will wake up for their rewards. The righteous will arise and be taken to heaven with the righteous who are still alive at His coming. Jesus spoke of the resurrection in these words: "Marvel not at this: for the hour is coming, in the which all that are in the graves shall hear his voice, and shall come forth; they that have done good, unto the resurrection of life; and they that have done evil, unto the resurrection of damnation" (John 5:28, 29).

The Bible teaches that there will be two resurrections. The first is of the righteous who will go to heaven with Jesus for one thousand years. Then Christ will return to this earth and resurrect the wicked who will be allowed to see why they received the sentence of eternal death.

The dead know nothing. They do not go anywhere. This is a clear Bible truth. The following formula provides a visual depiction of what the Bible teaches.

Dust + breath = living soul or being

Living soul – breath = dust

With all of this information it begs the question as to why people pray to dead saints who can't see, hear, or comprehend anything that is uttered in their name. But as in the Garden of Eden, Satan has trapped people with his lies. By performing miracles for people who pray to the Virgin Mary, Satan convinces people to continue the practice. Jerome Emiliani, born in 1481, was a prisoner and after praying to Mary, he was miraculously set free. Thereafter he dedicated his life to looking after abandoned children until he became the patron saint of orphans.

If we believe the Bible and the verses that state that the dead know nothing and are turned back to dust, then people can't be in purgatory or hell or heaven as some denominations teach. We've discussed what will happen to the righteous when Jesus returns to this earth, but what about the wicked who are alive at His second coming. Those who are wicked will die when they behold the dazzling glory of the King of kings and the Lord of lords. Unlike the wicked, the living righteous who welcome the Lord will be changed to immortal bodies, the kind of bodies Adam and Eve had prior to fall. In the meantime, the dead righteous, yes, only the dead righteous will be awakened. These resurrected ones will be drawn to Jesus who will be sitting in a glorious cloud in the sky. He will not set foot on the earth when He comes. After the resurrected saints meet Jesus in the clouds, the living saints will be drawn up. The saints will be in heaven for a millennium, and those thousand years will be a form of imprisonment for Satan who will be left on this earth with no one to deceive and play tricks on.

At the end of the thousand years, Jesus will return to this earth with the saints. He will descend with the New Jerusalem, which is in heaven now. At this time, the wicked dead will arise, and Satan will marshal them to attack the city of the saints. But before they can attack, fire and brimstones will shower on the wicked and the earth will turn into a lake of fire. This fire will burn all the unrighteous, the evil angels, and Satan. This will be the second death, which is eternal (see Rev. 20).

This massive fire will consume everything on the earth, and this earth will be made anew, and it will be called the new earth, which will be ideally designed for the righteous to live on forever. Jesus, in His Sermon on the Mount, said, "Blessed are the meek: for they shall inherit the earth" (Matt. 5:5). God's meek saints who preserved their faith in the face of persecution, imprisonment, and death are finally going to own this earth made new for them.

The writings of Paul confirm the sequence of the resurrection. "But I would not have you to be ignorant, brethren, concerning them which are asleep, that ye sorrow not, even as others which have no hope. For if we believe that Jesus died and rose again, even so them also which sleep in Jesus will God bring with him. For this we say unto you by the word of the Lord, that we which are alive and remain unto the coming of the Lord shall not prevent them which are asleep. For the Lord himself shall descend from heaven with a shout, with the voice of the archangel, and with the trump of God: and the dead in Christ shall rise first: Then we which are alive and remain shall be caught up together with them in the clouds, to meet the Lord in the air: and so shall we ever be with the Lord. Wherefore comfort one another with these words" (1 Thess. 4:13–18).

This clear truth stands triumphant over fallacies that have been taught by many denominations over the years, fallacies that are based on the lie that the devil told Eve in the Garden of Eden. He told her, "Ye shall not surely die" (Gen. 3:4). Many well-meaning preachers repeat these words to console the bereaved in believing that their dear loved one has gone to a better place and is in heaven looking down on them. But in uttering these words, the original lie that plunged humanity into sin is perpetuated. By believing that the dead are actually alive in heaven or hell opens up a vast world of supernatural evil activities connected to sorcery.

The Catholic Church promoted the humble mother of Jesus to sainthood, which was exactly what the devil schemed to accomplish. Church leaders carried out the deception the devil desired. If he could bring the mother of Jesus to an elevated position, he could divert all eyes from God to her. The worship that only belongs rightfully to God shifted to a created being instead of the Creator. Today the Catholic

Church has thousands of saints, and among them Mary is the first and most influential figure because of her relationship to Jesus.

Satan sought to destroy Jesus during His earthly life, but Jesus was victorious over sin and the grave. After Jesus' ascension, the devil turned his hatred to Christ's church in the form of persecution at first and deception later. Persecution strengthened and united the church, but deception eroded her morale and principles.

False teachings spread in the early church, but the apostles gave warning after warning to the church members. After their deaths, the local churches were under bishops, and false doctrines began to steadily creep in to the church. Thus a saint was lifted up who none would dare to challenge for the fear and honor of Jesus. Saint Mary was presented as an easy way to access God. People were told that even God is obliged to listen to her since she is the mother of Jesus. False doctrines thrive where there is no truth available, and since the clergy were the only ones who were allowed to read the Bible, the common people could not verify the truth or error of these doctrines.

"How rapidly the work of corruption progresses! What a contrast in color between this symbol and the first one: A black horse—the very opposite of white! A period of great darkness and moral corruption in the church must be denoted by this symbol. By the events of the second seal the way was fully opened for that state of things to be brought about which is here presented. The time that intervened between the reign of Constantine and the establishment of the papacy in A.D. 538 may be justly noted as the time when the darkest errors and grossest superstitions sprang up in the church. Of a period immediately succeeding the days of Constantine, Mosheim says:

" 'Those vain fictions, which an attachment to the Platonic philosophy and to popular opinions had engaged the greatest part of the Christian doctors to adopt before the time of Constantine, were now confirmed, enlarged, and embellished in various ways. Hence arose that extravagant veneration for departed saints, and those absurd notions of a certain fire destined to purify separate souls, that now prevailed, and of which the public marks were everywhere to be seen. Hence also the celibacy of priests, the worship of images and relics, which in process of time almost utterly destroyed the Christian religion, or at least eclipsed its luster, and corrupted its very essence in the most deplorable manner. An enormous train of superstitions was gradually substituted for true religion and genuine piety. This odious revolution proceeded from a variety of causes. A ridiculous precipitation in receiving new opinions, a preposterous desire of imitating the pagan rites, and of blending them with the Christian worship, and that idle propensity which the generality of mankind have toward a gaudy and ostentatious religion, all contributed to establish the reign of superstition upon the ruins of Christianity" (*Daniel and The Revelation,* p. 434).

When the doctrine that the dead go to heaven or hell was introduced to the Christian church, she was ready to accept it with no resistance or inquiry because the church had been weakened of her early principles and resolves. The worship of saints is the worship of the dead, which clearly goes against the Bible, and its teachings regarding the state of the dead.

Chapter 6

Idol Worship

——⟨ɷɷ⟩——

"The men of that generation were not all, in the fullest acceptation of the term, idolaters. Many professed to be worshippers of God. They claimed that their idols were representations of the Deity, and that through them the people could obtain a clearer conception of the divine Being" (*Patriarchs and Prophets*, pp. 95, 96).

That was how they defended their practice of wrongdoing, which is going on in a grander scale today. I have heard the excuse again and again that they really do not worship the statue, but the saint represented by it. But in this statement, I believe there are two wrongdoings, instead of one: 1) worshipping an idol of a saint; 2) worshipping a dead person considered to be a saint.

Throughout history people have preferred to have a tangible god, so people made gods out of a variety of materials. That's why people worshipped the trees, rocks, hills, sun, moon, stars, and animals. But worship of a visible object goes against the law of God.

The Ten Commandments, written by God's own finger,

state that God is the only God, and He is a living God. The first commandment says, "I am the Lord thy God, which have brought thee out of the land of Egypt, out of the house of bondage. Thou shalt have no other gods before me" (Exod. 20:2, 3).

The singularity of God is of supreme importance. The monotheistic doctrine was communicated to the first couple in the Garden of Eden. They rejoiced in the worship of the true God, and everything went smoothly for an unknown length of time until a third person, the devil, intruded into the relationship and introduced doubt and the belief that God isn't always right.

So it was that the children of Israel left Egypt and began their journey to the Promised Land with Moses as their guide. Along the way God reintroduced Himself to His people and gave them guidelines to live by. But they had much to learn. While Moses was up on the hill with God for forty days, the idolatrous people lost sight of whom they were worshipping, and they made a golden calf that they could see to worship, for they had participated in idol worship with the Egyptians. This act robbed God of what solely belongs to God—adoration from His created beings.

Thus, the second commandment specifically addresses the folly of idolatry. "Thou shalt not make unto thee any graven image, or any likeness of any thing that is in heaven above, or that is in the earth beneath, or that is in the water under the earth. Thou shalt not bow down thyself to them, not serve them: for I the Lord thy God am a jealous God, visiting the iniquity of the fathers upon the children unto the third and fourth generation of them that hate me; and shewing mercy unto thousands of them that love me, and keep my commandments" (Exod. 20:4–6). The golden calf incident was the first violation among God's people on the way to the land He had promised them.

The commandment clearly states that people must not bow down to idols or worship them. However, as we see in many churches and shrines, people habitually bow down to idols. They may say they really do not worship idols, but by bowing down, they have violated the second commandment. And as we learned earlier, the Catholic Church corrected the problem of violating this commandment by removing the entire commandment, which is noted in prophecy. "And he shall speak great words against the most High, and shall wear out the saints of the most High, and think to change times and laws" (Dan. 7:25). The papacy changed God's law by removing the second, changing the fourth, and splitting the tenth commandment to fit their doctrines and beliefs.

The apostle Paul began his epistle to the Roman church with a warning regarding worship. There he says: "Because that, when they knew God, they glorified him not as God, neither were thankful; but became vain in their imaginations, and their foolish heart was darkened.... Who changed the truth of God into a lie, and worshipped and served the creature more than the Creator, who is blessed for ever. Amen" (Rom. 1:21–25).

Catholics have a saint by the name St. Francis Zavier. This great Roman Catholic missionary converted pagans by the thousands. A student of Ignatius of Loyola and one of the first seven Jesuits, Francis Zavier engaged in soul winning in lands under Portuguese rule. He served in India, Japan, Borneo, the Moluccas, and many other areas where Christianity was not known. His service in India was very successful, but in other countries his pioneering ministry was slow as he had to first learn the language to preach. Born in Spain and educated in France, he first served the church in Italy. Francis then spent some time in Portugal before boarding a ship to India as a missionary. From there he went to Ceylon (Sri Lanka) too. His arduous journeys won a large number of Asians to Jesus.

The interesting thing I want to present is this. This great missionary was against idolatry, but it was the idolatry of pagan religions that he despised. He didn't seem to acknowledge that the Roman Catholic Church was also worshipping idols. He called the Hindus devil worshipers, and he asked his converts to abhor the statues and temples of their gods. In India he was the head of St. Paul's College, and he encouraged his students to destroy the statues of the pagan gods in their homes. He destroyed others idols while allowing the idols of his own church.

The Catholic ten commandments that Francis Zavier taught did not ban idol worship. And yet he hated the idols of other religions and condemned their gods. He abhorred the pagan idols but introduced converts to Catholic idols. As for God, all idols must be abhorred irrespective of the origin of religion. "For all the gods of the nations are idols" (Psalm 96:5). We are not to get into altercations with others by condemning their gods or idols. Instead, we are to let our worship be an example to others.

God says that He is a jealous God (Exod. 20:5). We know that jealousy is not a good thing, but jealousy pops up where love is strong. This jealousy is totally different from human jealousy of someone's possessions, achievements, success, etc. God becomes jealous when His people turn to other gods and worship them. If compared to a human perspective, lovers turn jealous when they sees the person they love so much loving another, and babies turn jealous when their mom takes another baby into her arms. This jealousy is a natural feeling. The stronger the love, the more aggressive is the jealousy. God is not ashamed to say that He is jealous, and we are not ashamed to say that we jealously guard our loved ones. In this sense, we cannot blame God for getting jealous.

"'I the Lord thy God am a jealous God.' The close and sacred relation of God to His people is represented under the figure of marriage. Idolatry being spiritual adultery, the displeasure of God against it is fitly called jealousy" (*Patriarchs and Prophets*, p. 306).

As you look at the Ten Commandments, the second and the fourth are more detailed than the other eight for a reason. The reason is that these two commandments—dealing with idolatry and the Sabbath—are crucial. Sadly, the Catholic Church, which is represented by the little horn in Daniel, tampered with both of these commandments.

If you walk into a Catholic book store, you inevitably see some statues for sale. Among them, Mary's statues are more common than that of other saints. Worship of Mary is ingrained in the hearts of Catholics—I should know because I was a Catholic myself. Mary easily wins the hearts of worshippers mainly because of her relationship to Jesus. Most worshippers do not know that every time they bow down to the idol or icon they are displeasing God by committing idolatry.

Marian worship was not present in the first century, but within a short period of time Mary emerged insuppressible, and she continues to gain more reverence and popularity. The seventh century was a very favorable period for Marian worship. The approval and support extended by Pope Sergius to conduct feasts in honor of Mary released new vitality to the passive devotion offered to the mother of God. It is interesting to note that much of the Marian hype was seen in the nineteenth century. The Feast of the Immaculate Conception commenced in 1854, which is a holy day of obligation. The Annunciation is another important feast held in her honor.

This is celebrated on March 25, in recognition of the date of conception of Jesus, which is exactly nine months before Christmas.

The specific date for the birth of Jesus is not found anywhere in the Bible or in contemporary historical documents. December 25 was chosen for the celebration of the birth of Jesus about four centuries ago to match an existing pagan holiday to make it easier for pagans to convert to Christianity. Interestingly, the church fathers of previous centuries picked different dates for the birth of Jesus. Clement said it was on November 18. Some others were of the opinion that Jesus was born on March 28. In the end December 25 was selected, even though it goes against the logic of the Bible story and these clues:

Zacharias belonged to the eighth division of priests to serve in the temple, down through the centuries it was known as the division of Abijah (1 Chron. 24:10; Luke 1:5). Bible scholars agree that the division of Abijah, according to historical calculations, served between June 13–19 in our present day calendar. It was during his time of service that an angel informed Zacharias that he was going to be a father (Luke 1:8–13). Assuming his wife conceived at the end of the month of June, we may guess that the child (John) was born in the end of March of the following year. When Elizabeth conceived, she kept herself in seclusion for five months. In the sixth month (December), Mary was informed of the conception of Jesus (Luke 1:26). This would indicate that Jesus was born in September according to our calendar.

September/October was the harvest time in that geographical area. After the harvest was secured, during the fair weather peasants were free to travel, making it easier to register for the census. Also, the Roman rulers would most likely not have inconvenienced their subjects by making them travel in the cold of winter in December.

Shepherds would not have been in the open fields with their flocks in the winter. And yet the Bible clearly documents that they were in the field.

The introduction of Christmas and the celebration of Jesus' conception were steps the Catholic Church took toward increased worship of Mary.

So how did the church, which was established by Jesus and promulgated by the apostles, develop into a tangled ramification of what we see today? There are approximately 41,000 Christian denominations today that have broken off of the true Christian church that Jesus established and the apostles built in the first century.

First, two churches branched off from the original church. The Assyrian Church separated after the Council of Ephesus in AD 431. Then in AD 451 the Council of Chalcedon took place, and another split resulted in the beginning of Oriental Orthodoxy.

The main Christian church proceeded, but it was severely weakened by false teachings and intruding traditions. By now the Christian faith had separated into three directions as shown above. Another split occurred in the eleventh century, resulting in two distinct names: Roman Catholic Church and Eastern Orthodox Church.

Then in the sixteenth century another major split took place. This split resulted when the powerful Roman Catholic Church lost believers to the European religious rebellion that is known as Protestantism. After that it didn't take long for Protestantism to divide into subgroups such as Anglicans, Lutherans, Presbyterians, Methodists, Baptists, etc.

Time marched on until the religious awakening that exploded in the early decades of the 1800s in North America. At this time a proclamation of genuine present day truth emerged. Bible students accurately calculated the time of a remarkable spiritual event based on the 2300-day prophecy of Daniel 8:14, but they mistook it to be the end of the world. When honest believers found out they were only a few years away from the appointed time, they were so excited that their impulsive preaching turned thousands of faithful ones from many different denominations to prepare for the second coming of Christ.

Each new denomination seemed to be formed to right the wrongs of the denomination they were splitting off of and return to the Bible. Unfortunately, today we are far from the original Christian church that Jesus established before ascending to heaven. We are far from the true worship of Christ; instead, as we have been discussing, idol worship has taken hold and the form of adoration to the saints and founders of the church.

"The darkness seemed to grow more dense. Image worship became more general. Candles were burned before images, and prayers were offered to them. The most absurd and superstitious customs prevailed. The minds of men were so completely controlled by superstition that reason itself seemed to have lost its sway. While priests and bishops were themselves pleasure-loving, sensual, and corrupt, it could only be expected that the people who looked to them for guidance would be sunken in ignorance and vice" (*The Great Controversy*, p. .57).

Jesus did not speak of saints who were living in heaven and should be worshipped. The idea of saints was instituted by the Roman Catholic Church for its own agenda. Those who venerate Mary regard her as their mediator to act in their behalf before God. Satan propagates this plan to sideline Jesus' role as Mediator. Some Catholic priests have even used the title "co-redeemer" to denote the important task

Mary is supposed to be fulfilling in heaven.

However, we know that we have only one Redeemer, and the Lord reminds us this fact through His Word. "I the Lord am thy Saviour and thy Redeemer, the mighty One of Jacob" (Isa. 60:16). Peter said by the inspiration of the Holy Spirit, "Neither is there salvation in any other: for there is none other name under heaven given among men, whereby we must be saved" (Acts 4:12). Also, "for there is one God, and one mediator between God and men" (1 Tim. 2:5).

Luke, the author of Acts, and Paul, the author of 1 Timothy, knew Mary well, and they never assumed that Mary was a co-redeemer or another mediator. These devilish attributions given to Mary emerged in the Dark Ages, and those who had no Bible knowledge or correct guidance, embraced the words of the priests as truth. Satan was keen that Mary be given all the honor and glory, because he wanted to blow Mary out of proportion, like Macy's jumbo parade balloons. He wanted her to appear bigger than God in the believers' eyes. Satan worked to set God's humble maid as a competitor against God. Mary, a woman who lived a humble life and no one knows the place she died, how she died, or when she died, has been turned into the queen of heaven.

And yet the Bible is clear as to the worship of idols. "The second commandment forbids the worship of the true God using images or similitudes. Many heathen nations claimed that their images were mere figures or symbols by which the Deity was worshiped, but God has declared such worship to be sin. The attempt to represent the Eternal One by material objects would lower man's conception of God. The mind, turned away from the infinite perfection of Jehovah, would be attracted to the creature rather than to the Creator. And as his conceptions were lowered, so would man become degraded" (*Patriarchs and Prophets*, p. 306).

The second commandment is based on total dedication to God who asks us not to stoop to the low level of worshipping any likeness of anything that is in heaven, earth, or in the water. Our Creator God is a living Being. We do not need to doubt His presence or awareness of what is going on. We can address our God directly, knowing very well that He hears us. We do not have to pray to a statue or an image to be heard.

None can take the place of God, the Creator of the universe. The first commandment says, "Thou shalt have no other gods before me" (Exod. 20:3). This recognition demands loving Him with all our heart, soul, and mind as explained by Jesus in Matthew 22:38. When we first love Him with all our heart and we have no other gods before Him, we should naturally cease to worship idols in adherence to His command.

Worship of God must be accomplished in spirit and truth, for God is Spirit (John 4:24). This is a direct heart-to-heart connection that does not allow for any likenesses in between. Jesus pointed out that "the true worshippers shall worship the Father in spirit and truth: for the Father seeketh such to worship him" (verse 23). He wants His worshippers to worship Him directly.

Idolatrous pagan gods are known for specific powers and blessings. Some worship a certain god for fair weather while others go to their god for protection, productivity, fortune, or healing. Those who worship the invisible Creator God know that by worshipping the one true God they can pray to Him for all their needs. Worshippers of God have a relationship with Him. Pagan worshippers do not have a specific knowledge of their gods. Their worship is traditional and habitual. Their knowledge is based on what the previous generation believed; whereas, God's people have a clear understanding of God. This understanding of God leads them to live by the

Ten Commandments given to them. "He that saith, I know him, and keepeth not his commandments, is a liar, and the truth is not in him" (1 John 2:4).

Nothing should come between our relationship with God and us. We are made in His image to commune with Him. Saints, idols, images, etc. have no place in our relationship with God. Unfortunately, throughout history God's people have struggled with this. Although idolatry was not a problem to Jesus and the apostolic church in their time, the Israelites in the Old Testament engaged in idol worship during some periods of time when the spirituality of the nation was at its lowest ebbs. Some kings such as Ahab and even Solomon committed this abominable sin, and they suffered its consequences.

The Christian church that was established by Jesus taught basic Christian principles along with the divine law to the Gentiles. Thousands were converted, and they joined the church through baptism. Gentile believers in the newly formed churches were well grounded in the truth having been converted by the inspired preachers.

As the time passed, the Roman Catholic Church was influenced by the pagan legacies of some of the converts who didn't want to completely give up their evil ways. Thus, the Catholic Church lowered their standards and became popular among nonbelievers who found it easy to join the church while holding on to their pagan customs. Other churches in Asia Minor maintained the truths they learned from Scripture. Within a couple of centuries, the Catholic Church grew so unChristian in principles that they worshipped the idols of Peter and Paul. Gradually the idol of Mary was introduced to the great joy of the blinded church.

In many eastern countries, people go on pilgrimages to shrines irrespective of their faith. I have toured famous

Hindu temples and have witnessed some known Christians worship these decorated idols, for they are known to perform miracles. These nominal Christians who go to temples to offer flowers are no Christians at all, for God's people have a commandment that totally prohibits idol worship. God's people have a commandment that sets them apart as Christians. Satan cunningly urged the papacy to remove this vital command so that millions could be diverted to the path of destruction.

"The worship of images and relics, the invocation of saints, and the exaltation of the pope are devices of Satan to attract the minds of the people from God and from His Son. To accomplish their ruin, he endeavors to turn their attention from Him through whom alone they can find salvation. He will direct them to any object that can be substituted for the One who has said: 'Come unto Me, all ye that labor and are heavy-laden, and I will give you rest.' Matthew 11:28" (*The Great Controversy*, pp. 568, 569).

As Marian worship became popular, the world of art jumped on board. The paintings of Mary are innumerable. They present her as an attractive woman, although the Bible gives no indication as to her outer beauty, except just her inner beauty and her desire to follow God. That is the whim of the artistic brush. Sculptors created world-class statues of Mary that are capable of receiving unreserved adoration. Beautiful hymns, music, and chanting evoked the human attention. Great authors wrote world-class books in her name. Probably the most popular song about Mary—"Ave Maria"— was written in 1825, it is the heartbeat of millions thanks to its exceptionally touching composition. It has been a popular choice for liturgical and devotional celebrations.

Residents of civilized countries recognize the fact that not knowing the law is not an excuse for violating the law.

Unfortunately, Catholics defend their idol worship because the Catholic version of the Ten Commandments does not forbid it. But God wants lives fashioned according to the divine precepts as shown in the original Ten Commandments He gave at Mount Sinai to the children of Israel.

A former nun, Mary Ann Collins wrote the following in an article titled "Mary Worship? A Study of Catholic Practice and Doctrine": "Beginning in 1948 there was a series of apparitions of Mary in the city of Lipa. These apparitions were sometimes accompanied by showers of rose petals and other supernatural phenomena. They occurred in a convent. The local bishop personally experienced a shower of rose petals and thereafter supported the apparitions. The media mocked the supernatural events in Lipa and street vendors sold phony "holy rose petals." In response to the bad publicity, the Vatican sent a Papal Administrator to take over the diocese where the apparitions occurred. He replaced the bishop and the mother superior. The nun who saw the apparitions was forced to leave the convent. The nuns were ordered to destroy all materials associated with the apparitions, including a statue. The convent was sealed and the nuns were not allowed to talk to anyone outside the convent. An official Commission of Inquiry was convened, which unanimously ruled that the apparitions were not valid. However, they did not interview anybody who had personal, first-hand knowledge of the events. Several of the bishops who were part of the Commission of Inquiry stated on their deathbeds that the Papal Administrator had forced them to sign the verdict by threatening to excommunicate them if they did not sign it.

"After years of no longer being a Catholic, I attended a Catholic funeral. When I went into the church something hit me hard. It had always been there, but I had never noticed it before because I was used to it. There were statues of Mary and the saints. They looked solid, real, as if they represented people of power. Jesus only appeared as a helpless baby in Mary's arms, as a dead man nailed to a cross, and as little wafers of bread hidden inside a fancy box. Visually and emotionally the message was very clear - if you want real power, if you want someone who can do something for you, then go to Mary and the Saints."

The culture of idols is not a new thing. It has existed from the time of antiquity. It looks harmless, like kids' play. But idol worship is not kids' play; it is a serious case of disobedience to God's law. Worshipping idols is nothing but worshipping the dead, which is what Satan wants. It is a pity that the great apostles and Mary have been subjected to this humiliation in contrary to their character and their devotion to God.

The labyrinth of confusing devilish deceptions spreads out in endless ramifications before humanity. The state of the dead, hell, purgatory, saints in heaven, idol worship, and many related topics are interwoven in the deception of Mary worship. The main reason why these lies took root is that believers blindly followed the priests and other theologians, unable to verify for themselves the accuracy of Scripture because the Bible was not available to the laity.

It is on record that when Pope John Paul II was shot, while in the ambulance on the way to the hospital, he did not pray to God or to Jesus. Instead, he prayed to Mary. The papacy created Mary worship, and they depend on Mary for protection as much as their deceived congregants. When he recovered, he made a pilgrimage to Fatima to thank her. He used to say, "Totus tuus sum, Maria," which means, "I am all yours, Mary." The pope is very dependent on Mary. Was it Mary or Jesus or God or Joseph who preserved his life from an assassin's bullet? The pope, the leader of the Catholic

Church, clearly worships the dead, and the whole Catholic Church follows his lead. God pities His children who are still in this Babylon, and He asks them to "come out of her, my people" (Rev. 18:4).

Catholics have spiritual leagues, militias and such organizations, to promote saint worship. Jesus said, "I am the way, the truth, and the life: no man cometh unto the Father, but by me" (John 14:6). Sadly, the Catholic Church has ignored the words of Jesus and has attempted to open various avenues to access the Father in heaven. "Membership in the Militia means complete dedication to the Kingdom of God and to the salvation of souls through Mary Immaculate," said Pope John Paul II.

The apostle John wrote, "My little children, these things write I unto you, that ye sin not. And if any man sin, we have an advocate with the Father, Jesus Christ the righteous" (1 John 2:1). We have only one advocate, but the papacy introduces another one in the form of Mary, mother of Jesus, claiming that the godhead cannot say no to her requests.

The man who was a proponent of the Marianist Movement, Alfonsus de Liguori (1696–1787), wrote that "Mary was given ruler-ship over one half of the kingdom of God." This was presented in the height of the Dark Ages in which thousands of dissenters were slaughtered by the Catholic Church. He seems to be a reporter of heavenly affairs, but what he wrote was a fable that many believed to be the truth of heaven.

Pope Pius IX went as far to say that "our salvation is based upon the holy virgin." But the Bible tells us that "neither is there salvation in any other: for there is none other name under heaven given among men, whereby we must be saved" (Acts 4:12).

Catholic tradition and the veneration of Mary,

documented and verbal, is the backbone of their faith, and they boldly say that it is equal to the Bible in authority. Jesus condemned human traditions when the Jewish traditions were regarded above the Scriptures during His time.

"Then came together unto him the Pharisees, and certain of the scribes, which came from Jerusalem. And when they saw some of his disciples eat bread with defiled, that is to say, with unwashen, hands, they found fault. For the Pharisees, and all the Jews, except they wash their hands oft, eat not, holding the tradition of the elders. And when they come from the market, except they wash, they eat not. And many other things there be, which they have received to hold, as the washing of cups, and pots, brasen vessels, and of tables. Then the Pharisees and scribes asked him, Why walk not thy disciples according to the tradition of the elders, but eat bread with unwashen hands?" (Mark 7:1–5).

This kind of adherence to traditions stands strong in the Catholic Church, and the approval of the bishops is needed before anyone accepts a biblical doctrine. Hence, "millions of pilgrims go to shrines which honor apparitions of Mary. Every year fifteen to twenty million pilgrims go to Guadalupe in Mexico, five and a half million go to Lourdes in France, five million go to Czestochowa (Jasna Gora) in Poland, and four and a half million go to Fatima in Portugal. Special dates draw huge crowds. On August 15, half a million pilgrims go to Czestochowa. On October 13, a million people go to Fatima. On December 12, 1999, five million pilgrims went to Mexico to honor Our Lady of Guadalupe," wrote Collins.

As you will notice in this quote, Mary veneration is very strong in many countries and local adherents have different names for her. Following are the various names for Mary throughout the world:

- Albania – Mother of Good Counsel
- Mexico and Latin American countries – Our Lady of Guadalupe
- Angola – Immaculate Heart of Mary
- Argentina and Paraguay – Our Lady of Lujan
- Australia and New Zealand – Our Lady Help of Christians
- Bolivia – Our Lady of Copacabana
- Brazil, Equatorial Guinea, Corsica, Portugal, Tanzania, USA, Zaire – Immaculate Conception
- Chile – Our Lady of Mount Carmel
- Costa Rica – Our Lady of the Angels
- Cuba – Our Lady of Charity
- Dominican Republic – Our Lady of High Grace
- Ecuador – Most Pure Heart of Mary
- El Salvador – Our Lady of Peace
- France, India, Jamaica, Malta, Paraguay, South Africa – Our Lady of the Assumption
- Haiti – Our Lady of Perpetual Help
- Honduras – Our Lady of Suyapa
- Hungary – Great Lady of Hungary
- Luxembourg – Our Lady Comforter of the Afflicted
- Philippines – Sacred Heart of Mary
- Poland – Our Lady of Czestochowa
- Puerto Rico – Our Lady of Divine Providence
- Slovakia – Our Lady of Sorrows
- Solomon Islands – Most Holy Name of Mary
- Uruguay – Blessed Virgin Mary
- Venezuela – Our Lady of Coromoto

This type of worldwide veneration is not given to any other saint, just Mary. This unprecedented popularity as a saint has become an effective tool in the hand of the enemy. No other saint has as many annual feast days as Mary.

Worshipping God is to be done under strict guidelines given by God in the Bible. As our example, Jesus worshipped God alone, the Creator of the universe. In like manner, the early Christian church never made anything to resemble anyone—man, beast, fish, or bird—as an idol to worship, for they knew God and His commandments. When members of the church were deprived of the pure teachings of Scripture, they became vulnerable to the devil's attacks. Without the Bible church members were unfamiliar with the second commandment of God that speaks against idol worship. With their leaders worshipping idols, when idols were placed in the church representing the apostles, who would have vehemently opposed idol worship if they were still alive, the gullible church members traveled down the wrong path.

The word idol and its various forms (idols, idolater, idolatry) occur 119 times in the King James Version Bible. Not only does the Bible plainly show God's stance on idol worship in the Ten Commandments, but texts and passages throughout the Old and New Testaments solidify God's law. Breaking the law is sin. Not knowing the law is no excuse. Let us review a few verses in which we hear God's words of admonition:

- "Turn ye not unto idols, nor make to yourselves molten gods: I am the Lord your God" (Lev. 19:4).
- "Ye shall make you no idols nor graven image, neither rear you up a standing image, neither shall ye set up any image of stone in your land, to bow down unto it: for I am the Lord your God" (Lev. 26:1).
- "And ye have seen their abominations, and their idols, wood and stone, silver and gold, which were among them" (Deut. 29:17).
- "And they served their idols: which were a snare unto them" (Ps. 106:36).

- "Their idols are silver and gold, the work of men's hands" (Ps.115:4).
- "Their land also is full of idols; they worship the work of their own hands, that which their own fingers have made" (Isa. 2:8).
- "Their idols are silver and gold, the work of men's hands. They have mouths, but they speak not: eyes have they, but they see not: They have ears, but they hear not: noses have they, but they smell not: They have hands, but they handle not: feet have they, but they walk not: neither speak they through their throat. They that make them are like unto them; so is every one that trusteth in them" (Ps. 115:4–8).
- "My people ask counsel at their stocks, and their staff declareth unto them ... and they have gone a whoring from under their God" (Hosea 4:12).

Paul often spoke of this evil that posed a threat to the pure faith. In 1 Corinthians 10:14 he wrote, "Wherefore, my dearly beloved, flee from idolatry." The city of Corinth was full of idols of pagan gods. Those who lived in that city were traditionally inclined to worship the idols and also to offer sacrifices to them.

Today, some seemingly worship the idol of this great apostle himself, Paul, who downright opposed idol worship. The Catholic Church in the adjoining city in my country is dedicated to Peter and Paul. Their massive statues are installed above the entrance to the city, and the bases of such statues in the churches are covered with flowers, offerings, and lit candles. Instead of fleeing from idols, these people worship the statue of the one who instructed all generations to do otherwise. The devil has blinded these people to the edifying instructions that they turn boldly against them. Some will argue that they are simply honoring the saints, but in most instances paying homage to the apostles has turned into worship.

In giving ourselves to God, we must give up all that will separate us from Him. Hence the Savior says, "Whosoever he be of you that forsaketh not all that he hath, he cannot be my disciple" (Luke 14:33). Whatever draws the heart away from God must be given up. "Mammon is the idol of many. The love of money, the desire for wealth, is the golden chain that binds them to Satan. Reputation and worldly honor are worshiped by another class. The life of selfish ease and freedom from responsibility is the idol of others. But these slavish bands must be broken. We cannot be half the Lord's and half the world's. We are not God's children unless we are such entirely" (*Steps to Christ*, p. 44).

God does not want partial dedication of heart. Christians are to give up their attachment to anything—money, worldly possessions, fame—or anyone—Mary, Peter, Paul—that they may be wholly His people. "He that loveth father or mother more than me is not worthy of me: and he that loveth son or daughter more than me is not worthy of me" (Matt. 10:37).

Worship of Mary has robbed the total undivided devotion God expects of His people. Catholics boldly say that the veneration of saints, including Mary, is not worship. Instead of examining the reason for the controversy, they hold the shield of defense to prove their point, for most of them cannot imagine the "mother of God" not being a central part of the church.

I remember once in my country how a young Catholic priest took steps to remove the statues out of his church. He was convinced of the second commandment of God's Ten Commandments that the worship of idols is totally against the will of God. He removed the statues of the saints, and his parishioners' reaction was quick. This took place in a village not far from mine. They approached him, puzzled and angry. Some of them rang the church bell nonstop. Ringing the church bell at an odd time was a message to the villagers that something has gone radically wrong. The roaring demands and the pressure made the priest place the statues back in the church.

The effects of the Catholic Church removing the second commandment and banning the reading of the Bible are playing out in the traditions that people now espouse to. Of course, all of this is a clear fulfillment of the prophecy that the papacy would "think to change times and laws" (Dan. 7:25).

But idolaters, beware! God clearly outlines a list of those who will be destroyed in the end (Rev. 22). They will be cast into the lake of fire and that will be their second death, which means annihilation forever. Among the destroyed you will see idolaters listed. There is no salvation for those who worship idols of any deity or saints instead of the true God.

Chapter 7

Prayer Beads

———

A string of beads has been associated with prayers since ancient times in such places as India, China, and the Middle East. We do not know how this invention came to the mind of the praying devotees who purportedly continued in this habit as a way of remaining connected to their deities through their long, chanting prayers. Many stalwarts in the Old Testament were known for their powerful, meaningful prayers, and Daniel stands tall among them. However, God's ancient people never resorted to using tools for their prayers. God instructed His people to share with Him their heartfelt thoughts and supplications.

In my travels through Nepal, especially in areas close to Tibet, I witnessed a different prayer tool used by those who came to the temple. One of their prayer tools is called a prayer wheel, which is a metal cylinder attached to a wooden handle. Prayers are engraved on the surface of the cylinder. Mere turning of the cylinder results in the offering of many prayers, according to their culture. These Tibetan artisans have invented these simple prayer tools to assist those who want an easy way to "say" prayers.

But mind you, that is not the end. They have gone tech savvy and produced solar powered prayer wheels that turn on their own. All you have to do is buy one for around $25 US and keep it in a sunny spot. They believe that the prayers keep ascending with no effort on their part. In order to give momentum to the spin, a metal weight is attached to the cylinder. Isn't it nice? Offering prayers without using one's lips are convenient, isn't it? And the solar prayer wheel enables the owner to earn merits even when sleeping. At each turn of the cylinder containing the prayer, according to their beliefs, it generates merits to the devotee. Tibetan prayer incantations are very soothing to the ear of the listener. The very same words are chanted nonstop for hours in their prayer sessions.

Prayer flags are another invention of these Himalayan inhabitants. Originally, prayers were carved on stones and wood blocks. Then they switched to writing on square or triangle pieces of cloth. These cloth prayer flags use the wind to offer prayers to their gods. As the prayer flag waves in the wind, they believe that the wind carries the written prayer to their deities.

In the 1940s and 50s records were very popular in my country. Some homes had a prestigious gramophone that played vinyl records for entertainment. Occasionally the gramophone needle stayed in the same groove, resulting in the same music or a few words playing again and again until someone picked up the needle arm and gently placed it on the turning record. This repetition of words was an annoyance to everyone listening. Do you think that God likes hearing recorded prayers again and again?

Repeating the same prayer does not mean perseverance in prayer. God's children should not present their prayers in a preset formula of words. Of course, our prayers may contain the same theme or request each time but in slightly different words.

The use of prayer beads among Hindus seems to have a history of about 3,000 or more years. Their prayer bead strings are known as malas. While praying, malas are used to help keep track of the number of times a prayer, mantra, chant, or the name of a deity is said. The length of the mala signifies how many times a mantra must be repeated. The longest mala contains 108 beads. Worshippers hold the beaded string in the right hand and move the beads between the thumb and the index finger as they repeat their prayers, which they believe delights their gods.

Scholars are of the view that prayer beads came to use around 8 BC in India. Hindus, Muslims, and Buddhists use this simple device in their incantation of repeated prayers. Among Christians, only Catholics adopted this age-old, ritualistic chanting system.

It has been discovered that medieval European Catholic monks and nuns used prayer strings in their solitary meditations—those isolated men and women were influenced by some traveling Hindus or Muslims who perhaps found lodging in their monasteries. Whatever the case may be, once introduced the practice of prayer beads and rote prayers emerged, and Pope Leo X gave his approbation to use prayer beads, known as the rosary, in 1520.

The prayer beads are used to keep track of the number of prayers offered to God. Why do they have to track of the number of prayers offered to God? Does God bless them according to the number of times they pray?

If we examine Scripture, our fathers offered humble prayers to God. Their prayers were warm in presentation and reflect the need of the moment. The prayer often began with praises to God for His goodness. Never were any of their prayers repeated word for word a few verses later.

Needs, situations, and the mood of the person offering the prayer constantly change; thus authentic and timely prayers are necessary, not repetitive mantras that are supposed to fit every situation. Christians believe in a prayerful heart that is connected to God all the time. When this connection is severed, even for a short while, inappropriate thoughts may creep in, endangering the believer to devilish temptations. Constant contact with God is not maintained by a mantra, but by sharing our humble thoughts with God as they originate in our mind.

I remember my confessions to the priest when I was in school. As an act of penance for some wrong act, he asked me to say three Hail Marys and three Lord's Prayers. Here I was repenting for hitting my brother and killing the neighbor's cat, but the words in my prayers didn't express any sort of repentance. Instead, I was made to repeat angelic salutations to Mary.

We were all excited in the month of May, which was especially dedicated to Mary. We set up a May altar in the classroom, as encouraged by the class master, and decorated it with fresh flowers. Mary's statue was on the top of it, and with her presence in the classroom, there was less noisy chatter and running about. Our prayers were directed to her at the beginning and end of school. I, too, had a date assigned to me to bring fresh flowers and a candle.

Jesus taught us to pray in His name, but after a few centuries, the Roman Catholic Church presented a more formidable personality to the believers and asked them to pray in her name. They promote that God is obliged to listen to her so things get done faster if you pray to Mary. Of course, this strategy is of the devil. He desires that all should forget about directly praying to God, who should be everything to His people.

Jesus instructed His disciples how to pray to God, giving us a model that presents the essential components a prayer should contain. Jesus gave us the Lord's Prayer, but He did not ask us to repeat it throughout the day verbatim. No, He taught us to talk to Him as to a friend. But the Catholic Church turned around and instituted Mary's Prayer. The devil duplicated God's efforts with his own design and suggested that the amount of times the prayer was said the more favor the person will have with God.

A rosary contains fifty-nine beads, and each bead stands for a prayer. Many Catholics are in the habit of saying the rosary three times a day. Worshippers who use the rosary offer prayers to Mary and a couple of Lord's Prayer to top it off. With statements of Scripture from the angel Gabriel and Elizabeth, Mary's cousin (Luke 1:28, 42), the Hail Mary prayer is as follows: "Hail Mary, full of grace. Our Lord is with thee. Blessed art thou among women, and blessed is the fruit of thy womb, Jesus. Holy Mary, Mother of God, pray for us sinners, now and at the hour of our death. Amen."

As you read the Hail Mary above, the question is, will the angelic salutation and Elizabeth's greetings help with guiding someone to the truth, healing in the sickness, protecting someone from harm, helping with one's studies, consoling the bereaved, asking for help with work or a life problem, seeking strength in weakness, requesting victory over sin, or recovering from loss. Each of these situations demands a prayer akin to its specific needs. That is why our prayers are variable as they should be so that God may know exactly what we need in each occasion instead of simply repeating Gabriel and Elizabeth's salutations.

The thief on the cross in utter agony offered a brief request to the Savior. His request turned out to be one of the most effective prayers recorded in the Bible, and the answer to His prayer came immediately in the form of assurance of salvation. Prayer should be one's own thoughts, originated in words that truly reflect the need of the moment.

Jesus, our only perfect example, prayed loud and clear in various situations, and as we analyze those words, it is easy to see how focused His words were to the need of the moment. His prayer life was constant, and throughout Scripture we see him praying publicly or in isolation, which shows His dependence on His heavenly Father. He didn't offer a cookie-cutter prayer, so why should we have one that'll take us nowhere.

The disciples saw their Master praying very often. As they followed Jesus day after day and watched Him pray, they asked Him to teach them how to pray. Prayers are infectious. Many have been positively impacted seeing someone bowing their head in silent prayer before eating at a restaurant. When Christians pray, those who see it also want to pray. But praying is not a mere chanting or repeating incoherent words. So Jesus willingly taught the disciples how to pray. One of the most important portions of the prayer is how Jesus started it. He began by addressing His heavenly Father. He did not say, "Our mother, which art in heaven." Jesus made it clear as to who we should be addressing.

There is no mother figure in Christian deity. Pagan's had goddesses, but not Christians. Greek and Roman cultural pressure and traditional views required a mother figure in the Catholic Church where many Gentiles found religious accommodation.

Jesus prayed directly to God the Father in heaven. He did not go through another person to commune with God.

The faithful believer does not need an in-between third person to communicate with God. In the Old Testament, sinners brought a lamb to the priest who intervened in a ceremonial ritual for the forgiveness of sins. It was a priestly ritual. However, these ceremonies were done away with when Christ died on the cross. Prayer or the communion with God does not need the support of an advocate. That communication line is always open for anyone, and it works much better than 9-1-1.

Jesus also taught us about appropriate prayers when He commented on two worshippers in the temple. One man offered a humble prayer with a contrite sinner's heart, while the other man boasted loudly, proclaiming his good qualities which was not like a prayer at all. The Savior's positive comment on the supplication of the silent devotee attested the approval of his prayer.

Jesus says that those who pray nonstop, repeating the same thing like parrots, are heathens. The prayer beads taken from the heathens created the heathen practice of repetition in prayers offered by those who hardly know the scriptural teachings. Jesus said, "When ye pray, use not vain repetitions, as the heathen do: for they think that they shall be heard for their much speaking" (Matt. 6:7). God's true church hangs on to its apostolic faith and practices while false religions make a mess of faith-related issues and adopt a whole lot of unChristian practices abominable to God.

Chapter 8

God's Law and His Saints

———◈◈◈———

The apostles and early Christians were strong in faith, and they left a legacy of living in the faith they accepted to future generations. Not that the early Christians did not have problems, questions, or even doubts about certain issues regarding the doctrines they learned, but they sought guidance from God and from His appointed servants. In such instances, they inquired of their elders to solve their doubts.

As the men and women of the early church learned more about doctrine and the Scriptures, they grew in faith. Their steadfast faith made them hold fast to their conviction in the face of torture and death. These people were regarded as saints, and we read of them in the book of Revelation. All those who have the truth of God and live by His principles as passed down since the Garden of Eden are saints of God, past and present.

Revelation classifies the saints so as to identify them

from the billions of nominal churchgoers. "Here is the patience of the saints: here are they that keep the commandments of God, and the faith in Jesus" (Rev. 14:12). God's people keep God's commandments—the Ten Commandments—as written by God with His own finger on two slabs of stone, which were given to Moses.

Unfortunately, many Christians follow a different set of commandments that were not designed by God. As we have discussed, the Catholic Church rewrote God's law without divine insight or approval. But this was not a random act of the papacy; God predicted this grave violation and the prophet Daniel wrote about it (Dan. 7:25). We must be careful to see the difference between the commandments of God and the commandments of man. God's commandments are found in the Bible (Exod. 20:2–17). God's saints observe these commandments, and by this obedience they are recognized as His people.

In an earlier chapter we discussed how the Roman Catholic Church removed the second commandment so as not to condemn idol worship. But that wasn't the only commandment they changed. They boldly admit to changing the law, which means they are openly disobeying God.

The following quotes document the Catholic Church's decisions to change the law.

"'Question: Which is the Sabbath day?'

"'Answer: Saturday is the Sabbath day.'

"'Question: Why do we observe Sunday instead of Saturday?'

"'Answer: We observe Sunday instead of Saturday because the Catholic Church in the Council of Laodicea (A.D. 336) transferred the solemnity from Saturday to Sunday'" (Peter Geiermann, *The Convert's Catechism of Catholic Doctrine,* p. 50).

Cardinal Maida, archbishop of Detroit, wrote in the *Saint Catherine Catholic Church Sentinel* on May 21, 1995, the following: "The holy day, the Sabbath, was changed from Saturday to Sunday ... not from any directions noted in the Scriptures, but from the Church's sense of its own power.... People who think that the Scriptures should be the sole authority, should logically become Seventh-day Adventists, and keep Saturday holy."

These two quotes are seen on the DVD titled *Signs and Wonders*. But those are not the only statements by the Catholic Church regarding the changing of God's laws. "The pope has power to change times, to abrogate laws, and to dispense with all things, even the precepts of Christ" (Decretal De Translat. Episcop. Cap.).

Notice these words in *The Catholic Record*, September 1, 1923, "Sunday is our mark of authority ... the church is above the Bible, and this transference of Sabbath observance is proof of that fact."

C. F. Thomas, chancellor of Cardinal Gibbons, wrote the following in November 11, 1895, in regards to the change of the Sabbath. "Of course, the Catholic church claims that the change was her act. And the act is a MARK of her ecclesiastical power and authority in religious matters."

The Jesuit Catechism says,

"Q. What if the Holy Scriptures command one thing, and the Pope another contrary to it?

"A. The Holy Scriptures must be thrown aside.

"Q. Who is the Pope?

"A. He is the Vicar of Christ, King of kings, and the Lord of lords and there is but one judgment seat belonging to God and the Pope" (Roy Livesey, *Understanding the New Age World Government and World Religion* [Chichester, England: New Wine Press, 1998], p.104).

"He falls and is lost who has not recourse to Mary. Mary is called the gate of heaven because no one can enter that blessed kingdom without passing through her. The way to salvation is open to none otherwise than through Mary ... He who is protected by Mary will be saved: he who is not will be lost.... God will not save us without the intercession of Mary" (Dave Hunt, *A Woman Rides the Beast*, p. 438).

The fourth commandment was changed by the papacy, making Sunday the Sabbath day instead of Saturday. But it did not pause there. Prophecy predicts that Sunday will be the mark of the beast and will be enforced before the end of the world. Sunday laws were enforced at some point and time in several states, but this enforcement will be world-wide, and it coming soon.

A declaration of COMECE, the Commission of the Catholic Bishops of the European Union, stated in January 2012, "It is the task of government to provide guaranteed market-free times and living spaces where people can search for ways to meet these needs. It is right that market activity is restricted on official public holidays and Sundays, because on those days, for national, cultural or religious reasons, peace and quiet and time to collect one's thoughts take precedence over economic activities."

Also in 2012, CNN posted the following article on their Web site: "To ring in the New Year, CNN's Belief Blog asked experts in religion, faith leaders, and a secular humanist about how the forces of faith and faithlessness will shape the world in 2012." The ninth entry, which was contributed by Jamie Korngold, rabbi and author of *The God Upgrade,* wrote this: "Sabbath becomes trendy! Fourth Commandment makes a come back! Sabbath named Time's person of the year! A new movement sweeps the country. They call themselves 24/6. Worn out by being tethered to the grid 24/7, sick of being accessible all hours of the day, inundated by updates, upgrades, and breaking news, Americans finally rebel, demanding, 'We need a day off.' People all over the country go offline for 24 hours every week. The simple break from the frenetic pace results in lowered cholesterol rates, fewer speeding tickets, and a reduction in marital strife. Peace, tranquility and contentment spread like wildfire" (CNN belief blog, "15 faith-based predictions for 2012" http://religion.blogs.cnn.com/2012/01/01/12-faith-based-predictions-for-2012/ [accessed November 25, 2012]).

In previous chapters we discussed how the Catholic Church removed the second commandment to enable idol worship and altered the fourth commandment to make it easier for Sunday observance. With only nine commandments, the church split the tenth commandment to make for a complete list of ten commandments. But these are not the original ten commandments, and the book of Revelation is very clear that the saints will keep the commandments of God, not of humans.

Jesus is coming soon. He is coming with thousands of angels. He is coming to take His saints to heaven, saints who lived and died on this earth and are asleep in the dust waiting His return. They will wake up at the voice of the archangel to join the living saints to be gathered to Jesus. At the second coming all the saints will receive their reward—eternal life with their Creator.

God's true believers have never had it easy on this earth. They are living in the devil's territory, and Satan hates God and His children. Jesus tasted this bitterness during His life on earth. This earth is no home to the saints. Threats, accusations, scandals, attacks, defamation, back biting, false charges, prisons, dungeons, chains, whips, nails, crosses, wild beasts, dens, plunder, loot, dispossession. All of these and more have been the share of the saints who are persecuted by Satan and his followers.

The saints of God stood firm before the sword and fire during the Roman Empire. They sealed their testimony with their blood when asked to recant their faith. They are asleep in the dust waiting for the voice of Jesus. The saints of the Dark Ages when the popes reigned supreme were tortured, killed, or plundered of their possessions and forced out of their lands. They lived in caves instead of in their homes. They were persecuted for 1260 years from AD 538 to AD 1798 as predicted in prophecy (Dan. 12:7; Rev. 12:6; 13:5).

Daniel, the beloved prophet of God, mentioned the kind of people who are God's loved ones. In his prayer he said: "O Lord, the great and dreadful God, keeping the covenant and mercy to them that love him, and to them that keep his commandments" (Dan. 9:4). Those who abide by the divine commandments show their true love to God. Jesus said, "If ye love me, keep my commandments" (John 14:15). Jesus kept the commandments as an example for us to follow (John 15:10). Saints keep the commandments of God; they are inseparable.

Some argue that Christ abolished the law—Moses' law, the ceremonial law, and God's law, the moral law or the Ten Commandments—and gave us only two commandments. Jesus said, "Thou shalt love the Lord thy God with all thy heart, and with all thy soul, and with all thy mind. This is the first and great commandment. And the second is like unto it, Thou shalt love thy neighbour as thyself. On these two commandments hang all the law and the prophets" (Matt. 22:37–40).

But Jesus debunks the myth that He came to destroy the law with this statement, "Think not that I am come to destroy the law, or the prophets: I am not come to destroy, but to fulfil" (Matt. 5:17). Instead, Jesus fulfilled the ceremonial law in its types and shadows as the antitype, and He fulfilled His duties to God (the first four commandments) and His duties to humanity (the last six commandments) in perfect obedience.

The original Ten Commandments are eternal. God gave the Ten Commandments to His people to live a life without sin and to please Him. But as the Catholic Church came into power, they allowed for the mixing of cultures and other religions. The Greek influence is evident in their architectural and religious legacy. Hellenistic gods and goddesses were worshipped in Roman temples under new names. Idol worship was rampant and quickly became the norm in Rome. By this time, the pure Christian principles had been compromised and nominal Christians had accustomed themselves to the social, political, and religious customs of the current age.

Many pagans joined the church, but church leaders did not stand firm and require that the new converts leave their pagan ways behind. Thus the pagans became Christians with most of their pagan habits intact. And slowly over time pagan practices slipped into the church until the church was pushed to change the commandments of God to match the new practices of the church. With the command that banned idol worship gone, believers were free to violate other commandments and fall deeper into sin.

Satan has diverted the attention of generations of people away from God and toward statues of saints who neither hear prayers nor offer salvation and the forgiveness of sins. Thousands upon thousands of people have blindly followed the example of the priests and committed idolatry within the church and at home based on the word of the Catholic Church. Sadly, every single one of them has broken or is still breaking the second commandment. Some may ask, could the breaking of one commandment out of ten be that destructive? Yes, the Bible clearly teaches that "for whosoever shall keep the whole law, and yet offend in one point, he is guilty of all" (James 2:10).

The "saints" who are canonized by the Catholic Church are subjected to several criterion to determine whether a dead person is a saint who has gone to heaven after death and should be idolized or not. The rules include:

1. Martyrdom
2. Asceticism
3. Renunciation of possessions
4. Lifelong dedication to the poor

The Catholic Church recognizes her saints in three scopes. The church militant comprises the living faithful believers. The church triumphant are those already in heaven. Then the church penitent comes next. They undergo a course of preparation for heaven in an imaginary place called purgatory. Of course, the first person elevated to the sainthood was Mary because of her relationship to the Lord. With Mary the Catholic Church, thus, commenced packing off the dead to "heaven" and honoring them after they died. The damage this malpractice has done to the Christian faith is irrevocable.

With the recognition of Mary's sainthood, the list grew rapidly with Stephen's name being subsequently added. Stephen, the brilliant first century preacher, was on fire with the inspiration of the Holy Spirit, but those who opposed him and the message of the risen Savior succeeded in their wicked plans, and they murdered Stephen in cold blood by stoning him. This was the first martyr who gave his life for Christ.

The ninth statement in the Apostles' Creed is as follows: "I believe in the holy Catholic Church: the communion of saints." The eleventh statement in the creed states, "I believe in the resurrection of the body." The question I have is this: How can the Catholic Church teach that good people go to heaven at their death but that there will also be a resurrection? If the dead are already in heaven or on the way to heaven through the transit station of purgatory, what is the use of a resurrection?

As more people were honored with the title of saint after their death, the idea of seeking favors from them naturally evolved. Believers were encouraged to pray to the saints for help with health problems, work, school, etc. In a sense the Catholic Church has turned heaven into a call center with many agents, or saints, waiting to listen to the supplicants. Of course, on this earth, parishioners not only pray to the saints but they also light candles and bring offerings of cash, flowers, and other things in an effort to express their gratitude for answered prayers.

The popularity of Marian worship and the enterprise of merchandise for sale and the offerings brought to Mary resulted in large financial gains for the Catholic Church. With this success, more and more saints were canonized and other merchandise, such as the rosary, was introduced. The Catholic Church has become a saint production machine. They say they don't create saints but only recognize them through the process of canonization, but the financial benefits that the church experiences is hard to ignore.

Canonization is indeed a long process. The church waits for a number of years to consider commencing the process on selecting a dead person for the honor of becoming a saint. The bishop of the area begins this work as an investigation after receiving permission from the Vatican. He appoints a tribunal to carry out the investigation, and they gather information from those who knew the dead person well to ascertain good qualities, virtues, and all good deeds, etc., of the person. At this time, relevant documents are collected to build the case. Once completed, the report goes to the Vatican officers, and they in the end pass it into the hands of the pope. Before the final proclamation of sainthood, at least two miracles need to occur within a set time period.

What are these saintly miracles? Although the Bible teaches that the dead know nothing, many people pray to dead persons in hopes that they will answer their prayers. The world is looking for wonders and sensationalism. People want a religion to cater to this need. Passive, humble, and graceful worship is not recognized anymore. Like Herod who hoped that Christ would perform a miracle before his eyes (Luke 23:8), many seek miracles to confirm their allegiance to a saint or God Himself. People want a live, performing religion. They are ready to worship those who prove their power and worth by performing miracles.

The dead are really dead, but Satan, the impersonator, is very much alive. He knows the gains he can make in tricking people by performing miracles in the name of dead "saints." He tricked Eve in the Garden of Eden with the assurance that she would not die. Yet Eve disobeyed and Satan was given a foothold. He has continued to trick humanity with the same claim that we will not die—there is something better waiting beyond the grave as soon as death occurs. By performing a miracle in the name of a dead person, his lie— you shall not die—is reaffirmed.

The danger of worshipping idols is that the worship is aimless. People are more prone to worship the tangible idols of their miracle-performing saints than God. In fact, many people who worship saints do not pray to God anymore. They turn their attention away from seeking God with all their heart, understanding, soul, and strength (Mark 12:33) and falsely follow Satan. This formula found in Mark 12:33

is plainly presented by Jesus throughout the Bible, but so many people do not follow God's clear directives.

The devil did not force Eve to eat the fruit, nor does he force anyone to worship idols. When he tempts us, we must decide whether we will obey God or listen to Satan's lies. Lot's wife was told not to turn around, but she did. Eve was told not to eat the fruit, but she did. Moses was told not to strike the rock, but he did. None of them was spared the consequences. God says obey, and Satan says disobey. Jesus taught that the dead are asleep, but Satan tells the world that the dead are in heaven. Satan's lies have cost millions of people their eternal reward. He is truly "a liar, and the father of it" (John 8:44).

Saints are holy people who live according to God's commandments, but they are not in heaven, for this teaching is directly contrary to the Bible. As we study this topic, it is important to remember that we are judged by the law. As this is true in the civil court, it is true in the heavenly court. The judgment is occurring in heaven right now, and every person's life will be reviewed. The standard God uses to judge the world is His law, which He gave to Moses on Mount Sinai. When He says, do not do something, He means it. This is where our loyalty, faithfulness, and sincere love are tested. A list of those who will not enter heaven is found in the Bible—among those are idolaters (Rev. 22:15).

Chapter 9

The Destruction of the Wicked

———◊◊◊———

The false teaching that those who are good go to heaven when they die has its seesaw effect on the wicked. It is taught that the wicked end up in hell and those who are only somewhat wicked end up in purgatory. The Bible speaks of hell many times and of eternal fire, and some people attend church out of fear of hell where it is preached that the unrighteous are screaming in utter agony as they are continually burned alive.

Those who ponder this aspect of punishment present two views about hell. Some say that God is love and He would never allow anyone to burn forever. Others hold the notion that the wicked deserve to be burned forever because of their crimes. Let me tell you the plain truth: there is no hell right now. As for purgatory, the whole notion is a lie.

God is love, and He longs that all would confess their sins, for He is faithful to forgive those who do (1 John 1:9).

But God also makes it clear that those who are too arrogant to repent and confess their wrongdoings will face the consequences of their sins: "the wicked shall not be unpunished" (Prov. 11:21). It does not please God to have to punish anyone, but divine justice cannot be ignored.

When Jesus took our sins on Himself, He was separated from God because God cannot be in the presence of sin. God couldn't intervene and save Jesus because divine justice required that the wages of death be paid for the sins of the world (Rom. 6:23). Jesus paid that price so that we could live. But those who refuse to accept Jesus' free gift of salvation must answer for their sins without the covering of Jesus' blood. "And I will punish the world for their evil, and the wicked for their iniquity" (Isa. 13:11).

As we learned from our study of the dead, both good and bad are in the ground—the righteous and wicked are sleeping in the grave. Just like we've learned that the good are not in heaven, the bad are not in hell. But the day is coming when the wicked will pay for their deeds in the eternal fire, or hell, that will consume them. But this is a one-time event. There will be hell with molten lava burning the wicked who have died since the beginning of time.

As previously discussed, when Jesus returns at the second coming, He will raise the righteous from the dead and gather the living righteous with them and take all those who are sealed for heaven home with Him. The righteous dead shall be resurrected in incorruptible bodies and at the same time the righteous living also will be changed. "Now this I say, brethren, that flesh and blood cannot inherit the kingdom of God; neither doth corruption inherit incorruption. Behold, I shew you a mystery; We shall not all sleep, but we shall all be changed, In a moment, in the twinkling of an eye, at the last trump: for the trumpet shall sound, and the dead shall be raised incorruptible, and we shall be changed" (1 Cor. 15:50–52).

For one thousand years the righteous will live in heaven before returning to earth to witness the fate of the wicked who have all been sleeping in the grave while Satan has roamed the earth without anyone to tempt or torture.

The wicked will be burned alive; there is no question about it. The sure word of prophecy states that some will receive everlasting life, while others will awaken to eternal death (Dan. 12:2). Daniel wrote these words at the direction of the angel Gabriel. We can be assured that the words of Scripture will happen.

"But the heavens and the earth, which are now, by the same word are kept in store, reserved unto fire against the day of judgment and perdition of ungodly men" (2 Peter 3:7). The wicked dead are not in hell for there isn't a place called hell. The hellish fire that will destroy the wicked is to come after the thousand years that the righteous will spend in heaven.

During the Middle Ages when church members were not allowed to read the Bible for themselves, many fables and religious fabrications were presented by the clergy and monks to their gain. Eternal hell fire was one of those ideas. Then the falsehood of purgatory was presented to prompt the people of dead relatives to pay for requiem masses which they were told would assist in moving the deceased person from purgatory to heaven, instead of to hell.

The Bible presents a clear picture that goes against what is taught by the Catholic Church. After the wicked are raised to life, Satan will rally his troops and convince them to try and capture the New Jerusalem that is descending from heaven (Rev. 20:7–9). "And they went up on the breadth of the earth, and compassed the camp of the saints about, and the beloved city: and fire came down from God out of heaven, and devoured them" (verse 9). That is the beginning and the end of the lake of fire, which we call hell. Isn't it plain to understand the lie of an existing hell?

Not only is Revelation clear on the matter of hell, but the Old Testament prophets also pointed to a day of burning that was yet to come, not going on now. "For, behold, the day cometh, that shall burn as an oven; and all the proud, yea, and all that do wickedly, shall be stubble: and the day that cometh shall burn them up, saith the Lord of hosts, that it shall leave them neither root nor branch. But unto you that fear my name shall the Sun of righteousness arise with healing in his wings; and ye shall go forth, and grow up as calves of the stall. And ye shall tread down the wicked; for they shall be ashes under the soles of your feet in the day that I shall do this, saith the Lord of hosts" (Mal. 4:1–3).

The Bible is clear as to the destruction of the wicked by fire, but there are a few verses that mention an unquenchable fire, which seems to speak of something burning forever. Those who promote a physical place called hell reference these texts in support of their case. But let's examine them to understand their true meaning.

Jeremiah talks of an unquenchable fire in Jerusalem. "And it shall devour the palaces of Jerusalem, and it shall not be quenched" (Jer. 17:27). This prophecy was fulfilled, and its fulfillment is recorded in 2 Chronicles 36:19. The massive fire that engulfed the city palaces eventually burned out when the palaces were no more. Fire needs fuel. It lasts as long as there is flammable material available for it to consume, but it naturally dies down once there isn't anything left to burn. Jeremiah predicted that the fire in Jerusalem could not be quenched, and that was true. None could quench it. No one could extinguish it.

The hell fire that will consume the wicked will last as long as there is something to burn. Once everything is burned, the fire will go out. Jesus spoke of the everlasting fire this way: "Then shall he say also unto them on the left hand, Depart from me, ye cursed, into everlasting fire, prepared for the devil and his angels" (Matt. 25:41). The words Jesus used, "everlasting fire," meant an unending fire that will consume everything in its wake.

Now see what Jude writes: "Even as Sodom and Gomorrha, and the cities about them in like manner, giving themselves over to fornication, and going after strange flesh, are set forth for an example, suffering vengeance of eternal fire" (verse 7). The unquenchable fire that devoured those cities is no more, neither are the cities that were subjected to the "eternal fire." Jesus and other Bible writers commented on the eternal fire in the context of burning until the fire is extinguished. Others have taken their words literally and gotten lost in unbiblical theories about eternal fire.

Let's now turn to two texts in Revelation where John uses the phrase "for ever and ever."

"And the smoke of their torment ascendeth up for ever and ever" (Rev. 14:11). "The devil that deceived them was cast into the lake of fire and brimstone, where the beast and the false prophet are, and shall be tormented day and night for ever and ever" (Rev. 20:10).

John wrote in the Greek language, and they used this expression casually to mean an endless time. But when we look at other scriptures in context, we discover that "eternal fire" refers to a length of time necessary for the fire to do its job. Once the fire has consumed everything, it goes out according to the laws of nature.

The word forever is also used elsewhere in the Bible and sheds light on how the word is used and what it means.

"For perhaps he [the slave who escaped] therefore departed for a season, that thou shouldest receive him for ever" (Philemon 15). The slave would not live forever, but Paul is saying that the master could keep his slave for life. "Then thou shalt take an aul, and thrust it through his ear unto the door, and he shall be thy servant for ever" (Deut. 15:17). Once again, this means until the slave dies.

"Howbeit the Lord God of Israel chose me before all the house of my father to be king over Israel for ever" (1 Chron. 28:4). David only ruled for forty years, but the term forever meant until his death. "I went down to the bottoms of the mountains; the earth with her bars was about me for ever" (Jonah 2:6). Jonah's "forever" lasted three days.

Scripture is clear that the wicked will be consumed by fire and the earth will be cleansed by fire in order to completely eradicate sin once and for all. But that cleansing will not be a perpetual fire that will go on for eternity. Once the fire has consumed everything, the new earth will be created in place of the scorched earth.

Those who are faithful to God by abiding by His divine law have nothing to worry about in regards to hell or eternal fire. The good news is that there is a divine regime called heaven where the throne of our heavenly Father is, and hell is a term given to the eternal fire that will consume the wicked and cleanse the earth.

The state of the dead, idol worship, hell, and heaven are important subjects that must be properly understood so that we can worship God in spirit and in truth.

Chapter 10

Marian Visions

Jesus emphatically said, "I am the way, the truth, and the life: no man cometh unto the Father, but by me" (John 14:6). Satan knows this, so he found someone who could stir the hearts of those whose faith is not built upon Jesus, the Rock (1 Cor. 10:4). Venus, Diana, and other goddesses were perhaps more popular among the pagan worshippers than their male counterparts. This is the natural human tendency. Children are drawn to their mother, though they know well the ultimate provider is their father. The devil knows human psychology, and he has played upon it since the beginning of time.

In his early surveillance of humanity, Satan learned the weak points of the human race. Although created in the form of God, humanity was below the levels of angels in many ways, including wisdom. Satan, being an ex-angel, had an advantage over the first couple whose only safety depended on their loyalty and obedience to God. This, the devil knew, would be traded in if their ambitions and desires were stimulated by some compatible temptations. They had plenty to eat, so hunger was not a good tempter. They did not have parents, so there was no way for them to dishonor their parents. Murder was an impossible option for they were both immortal. In the absence of a third party, adultery was out of question. What about stealing? It was not a temptation to either of them, for they had been abundantly supplied to the brim. Bearing false testimony too was not a thing that could be done because they had none to listen to their lies. Coveting others spouses or donkeys too was out of the picture. Satan did not tempt them to break the last six commandments. Instead, he tempted them to break the divine-human relationship of the first four commandments—he tempted them to disobey God and question His word.

If Eve had moved away from the tree the minute the serpent addressed her, we would have enjoyed immortality, but she paused and entertained his question. She allowed herself to get caught up in the notion that she would have knowledge like God and would not die (Gen. 3:1–6).

Eve succumbed to Satan's temptation, and billions of her children have followed in her footsteps, falling for Satan's temptation that the dead are really not dead, they are in heaven, purgatory, or hell.

The devil has impersonated the dead since the fall, giving supposed credence to his lie. It is natural for human beings to miss their loved ones who have died, and many people dream of their deceased relatives.

At times I dream of my dead mother who has passed away, and I awake with happy feelings for having seen her and talked with her in my dreams, but I know that they are just dreams, nothing more. My mother is resting in the grave, not floating about as some spirit who can come back and interact with me.

Of course, Satan wants to convince people that seeing

their dead relatives is not a dream but is a real experience with someone beyond the grave. We have heard of apparitions and ghosts in the media. There are reports on TV of those who have seen ghosts and dead people who have come back. The books and movies that present eerie scenes and encounters with the dead are best sellers and box office hits. There is demand for this type of suspense thrillers. More than any time in the past, society is ready to see apparitions. For example, the *Ghost Hunters* TV series is regularly watched by millions.

This type of atmosphere sets the stage for Marian sightings. These have been documented, scrutinized, and shifted to retain a few that will stand the test of critics and opponents. Many claim to have seen Mary or received a message from her with the idea of becoming rich and famous. Sadly, the approved sightings are misleading the gullible. They say the Marian sightings are real, but how can they be real when Mary is dead and in the grave?

Apparitions of Mary looming over trees, church buildings, in the clouds, and such are plentiful. The mind has a way of playing tricks when we open ourselves up to the imaginings of the world and the things around us. Look at a stone wall, fall leaves, or the clouds and see how many apparitions you can visualize. The mind is innovative, imaginative, and also deceptive. The father of lies creates apparitions that appear, do things, and speak messages. Satan personifies the dead to support his original lie that "you will not die."

Miraculous sightings of apparitions have been recorded in every country, and they are not all of Mary. Some staunch Buddhist and Hindu countries have also been recipients of strange sightings. I have seen photos of Buddhist and Hindu shrines with peculiar flashing lights. They believe it to be the radiance of God or of the sacred relict. Who is the mastermind behind all these exhibitions? He is the prince of this world. Soon he will be cast out, but until then he continues to attempt to deceive the world.

In one apparition, Saint Catherine Labouré received a vision from Mary and the instruction to produce a medal, which was named the Miraculous Medal. The Catholic Church says that the medal is not a good luck charm, but they do claim that those who wear it will obtain special blessings. Upon her death, Catherine was beatified in 1933 and canonized in 1947. Everyone wanted to buy and wear the medal around their neck.

On May 13, 1917, Mary supposedly appeared to three children in Fatima, a small town in Portugal. Records indicate that she appeared a total of six times, identifying herself as "Lady of the Rosary." She counseled the children to do penance for their sins and the sins of others. Thousands of people flocked to the area where the apparition took place in hopes of receiving some blessing from being in the area where Mary supposedly appeared.

Life after death is fascinating to many. It is a secretive world of fantasies. As in the ancient times of Egypt, Babylon, and Persia with its magicians, soothsayers, astrologers, and interpreters, today offers a new breed of spiritualists. Through the Internet, you can have your palm read and horoscope checked. Computers do the calculations, but people believe the revelations as truth. There are millions of New Age and mystic sites waiting to serve those who want to dabble with the dark side.

King Saul in utter desperation tried to contact a spirit to find out about the outcome of the battle he was going to fight. He, who acted against the devilish spiritualism in his early reign, became so frustrated in God's silence, which was brought about by Saul's selfish choices, that he sought help from a witch who called the dead Samuel to speak with the king. The king saw a hazy figure like Samuel emerge from the earth, and he answered the king. It was not Samuel the prophet of God because he was already dead. Instead, it was Satan or an evil angel. Just as Satan was able to impersonate Samuel, he can impersonate Mary or even Jesus.

Therefore, we must watch and be ready lest we be fooled. Jesus told His disciples, "Behold, I have told you before. Wherefore if they shall say unto you, Behold, he is in the desert; go not forth: behold, he is in the secret chambers; believe it not. For as the lightning cometh out of the east, and shineth even unto the west; so shall also the coming of the Son of man be" (Matt. 24:25–27).

One verse later, Jesus said, "Immediately after the tribulation of those days shall the sun be darkened, and the moon shall not give her light, and the stars shall fall from heaven, and the powers of the heavens shall be shaken: And then shall appear the sign of the Son of man in heaven: and then shall all the tribes of the earth mourn, and they will see the Son of man coming in the clouds of heaven with power and great glory" (Matt. 24:29–30).

Do not be carried away by apparitions, sightings, miracles, and wonders of the last days. The Bible is clear as to the signs of Christ's coming and the state of the dead. Satan will do anything to keep you from the truth, and it is your responsibility to stay vigilant in the hour of temptation. "Be sober, be vigilant; because your adversary the devil, as a roaring lion, walketh about, seeking whom he may devour" (1 Peter 5:8).

The following timeline outlines the approved apparitions of the Roman Catholic Church:

1. Our Lady of Guadalupe – seen by Juan Diego in Guadalupe, Mexico, in 1531

2. Our Lady of Laus – seen by Benoîte Rencurel in Saint-Étienne-le-Laus, France, between 1664 and 1718

3. Our Lady of the Miraculous Medal – seen by Saint Catherine Labouré in Rue du Bac, Paris, in 1830

4. Our Lady of La Salette – seen by two shepherd children in La Salette, France, in 1846

5. Our Lady of Lourdes – seen by Saint Bernadette Soubirous in Lourdes, France, in 1858

6. Our Lady of Pontmain – seen by a number of young children in France in 1871

7. Our Lady of Fátima – seen by three shepherd children in Portugal in 1917

8. Our Lady of Beauraing – seen by five children in Belgium between November 1932 and January 1933

9. Our Lady of Banneux – seen by Mariette Beco in Banneux, Belgium, in the 1930s

10. Our Lady of Akita – seen by Sister Agnes Katsuka Sasagawa near Akita, Japan, in 1973

Of course there are other sightings that have not been approved by the church, including sightings in the United States. If you do an Internet search for Marian apparitions, you come up with a host of Web sites dedicated to sightings of the mother of Jesus.

Of course, the diabolical deception of the Catholic Church encourages people to try their luck in pretending to receive communication and messages from Mary, which has come back to bite them. Many people have found this to be an easy way to become influential and get rich. Such tricksters became a nuisance to the church, and the church has named their sightings as unauthentic. Some of those who made a fortune are Mary Jane Even, William Kamm,

Julia Kim, Vassula Ryden, Theresa Lopez, and others. The Catholic Church intervened in each of these events and proclaimed that such phenomenal activities lacked genuineness and credibility. According to church leaders, the claims of these individuals were contradictory to the church doctrines. Some of them pretended to be miracle performers and began issuing Marian messages, but they were told by the church that their messages were devoid of supernatural origins.

The New Age Movement has taken a strong hold in regards to Marian philosophy. Their special rosaries, which are blue, bring in a good profit. These are obviously quite different from the Catholic rosary, but the idea is the same that a series of prayers be offered in a specific order.

The rise of Marian worship came about in the Dark Ages when the people were cut off from the Bible. During this time, the devil ruled the minds of many and turned them toward superstition and spiritualism. The stark lies of the Roman Catholic Church easily took root in this atmosphere. As the church fell deeper into apostasy, the papacy finally declared itself infallible in order to justify all the deviations it was introducing contrary to the Bible.

What began as the early Christian church founded on the Rock, Jesus Christ, has morphed into standing on the papal foundation and the saints, such as Peter and the apostles. This is not my idea—it is true that Jesus said, "That thou art Peter, and upon this rock I will build my church" (Matt. 16:18), but Jesus was not literally referring to the fact that Peter would be head of the church to be worshipped and followed as a saint. "You are a stone, and upon this rock (1 Corin.10:4) I will build my church." Panicky short tempered Peter proved many times to be more of an unstable stone than a rock. There were other apostles who were more composed than Peter.

Jesus shared with His disciples the fact that He would be killed and raised to life in three days. But Peter, in his bold manner and selfish human nature, rebuked Jesus and said, "Be it far from thee, Lord: this shall not be unto thee" (verse 22). Jesus immediately responded, "Get thee behind me, Satan: thou art an offence unto me: for thou savourest not the things that be of God, but those that be of men" (verse 23).

Peter could not stand the thought of the Master suffering and dying, so he sought to convince Jesus that He didn't know what He was talking about. Then when Jesus' prophecy did come true, Peter panicked and cut off the ear of a servant in the mob. Finally, he struggled to stand in the midst of the trial, and he denied Christ. But that isn't the end of Peter's story.

The book of Acts records a transformed Peter after the anointing of the Holy Spirit at Pentecost, and he preached to a very large crowd and converted thousands in one day. Although Peter took an active leadership role in the early Christian Church, there is no evidence that he placed himself above the other apostles or church leaders. He worked in conjunction with the other apostles to guide the fledgling church (Acts 8:14; 15:6; Gal. 2:11).

It was the Catholic Church that pushed Peter to a position of importance by suggesting that he was the first pope, reigning from AD 32–67, and yet there is no biblical record of any such title being bestowed upon Peter. Furthermore, the Bible does not sanction or document the formation of the Catholic Church as should have been recorded if Peter was chosen as the first pope. Such an event would surely be included in the chronicles of the early Christian church.

The first ten popes of the Catholic Church are listed as follows:

1. St. Peter, AD 32–67;
2. St. Linus, AD 67–76;
3. St. Anacletus, AD 76–88;
4. St. Clement I, AD 88–97;
5. St. Evaristus, AD 97–105;
6. St. Alexander I, AD 105–115;
7. St. Sixtus I, AD 115–125;
8. St. Telesphorus, AD 125–136;
9. St. Hyginus AD 136–140;
10. St. Pius I, AD 140–155.

Interestingly, in other Christian records, the following names are listed as the early church fathers: Clement of Rome, Ignatius of Antioch, Polycarp of Smyrna, Irenaeus of Lyons, Clement of Alexandria.

The Dark Ages and the removal of the second commandment by the Catholic Church opened the door to the worship of saints, which in turn opened the door for Marian visions. These decisions led to other unbiblical practices such as priestly confessions, selling indulgences for the forgiveness of sins, and acts of penance, encouraging church members to beat themselves with scourges to pay for their sins.

Among other unbiblical errors of the Dark Ages, the Catholic Church instituted prayers directed toward Mary and other saints; kissing the Pope's feet, worshipping the cross, relics, and images; use of the rosary; inquisition; sale of indulgences; and purgatory. The church also took the Bible away from the members, added six books to the Bible, and proclaimed the infallibility of the pope.

Mary, the blessed mother of Lord Jesus Christ is worthy of our adoration for her part in the plan of salvation, by accepting the motherhood of the Redeemer. Her care of this special Child is an example to all mothers. Her humble decision to follow God's will in the face of social pressure is a lesson of sacrifice. She sacrificed her name and was rewarded with raising the Son of God. But after her service was over, like Joseph, she faded away into obscurity. She never thrust herself into the limelight nor requested praise and adoration for her role in the Savior's life. The devil is the one who developed this scheme.

The Bible is clear about the state of the dead, idol worship, and heaven and hell, but one must read the Bible and believe it in order to make a change and distance oneself from the false doctrines of the Catholic Church. I have no intention of hurting the feelings of those of the Catholic faith, for I have many relatives and friends who still practice Catholicism. However, the truth must be presented. Those who wish to be saved can do so only be coming to Jesus, who is the way, the truth, and the life. A clear knowledge of Scripture is crucial for one's salvation, for it leads sincere Christians into all truth.

We live in the last days, and we must stand strong against the devil's deceptions, which includes the veneration and worship of Mary. It is my prayer that you may accept the truths presented in this book. If you are seeking additional materials along this same subject line, I encourage you to read *National Sunday Law* by Jan Marcussen, which is available through TEACH Services, Inc.

We invite you to view the complete
selection of titles we publish at:

www.TEACHServices.com

Scan with your mobile
device to go directly
to our website.

Please write or email us your praises, reactions,
or thoughts about this or any other book we publish at:

TEACH Services, Inc.
P U B L I S H I N G
www.TEACHServices.com ⚫ (800) 367-1844

P.O. Box 954
Ringgold, GA 30736

info@TEACHServices.com

TEACH Services, Inc., titles may be purchased in bulk for
educational, business, fund-raising, or sales promotional use.
For information, please e-mail:

BulkSales@TEACHServices.com

Finally, if you are interested in seeing
your own book in print, please contact us at

publishing@TEACHServices.com

We would be happy to review your manuscript for free.

CPSIA information can be obtained at www.ICGtesting.com
Printed in the USA
LVOW012343130213

319917LV00001B/4/P